A Brewerytown Kid Grows Up

A Brewerytown Kid Grows Up

Michael J Contos

Aka **Contoveros**

I grew up in a tough neighborhood of Philadelphia and learned how to sing and dance as well as box at my elementary school. I served as an altar boy at church and remember getting my first French kiss at age 12 while experiencing the Presence of God while praying that the girl I met the night before would like me a little.

The group I sang Doo Wop with appeared on television and we were once offered a contract to sign two songs on an LP. It was the greatest regret of my life when members of our singing group held out for more money and we were never given another chance to record.

I got drafted the same day that Billy Joe McAllister jumped off the Tallahatchie Bridge. (See Bobby Gentry's song *"Ode to Billy Jo!"*) My brother George, who was a "lifer" in the army, convinced me to go to OCS -- Officers Candidate School -- and I ended up leading a combat infantry platoon in Vietnam. I used the teachings I learned from the old neighborhood – Brewerytown – and kept all my troops alive even though I ended up being blamed for a friendly fire episode that haunted my life from age 21.

Feeling I failed in the Vietnam War, I propelled myself in studies at a community college and then a university where I got a bachelor's degree in journalism and a masters' degree in American history. I was fortunate to work as a newspaper reporter shortly after Bernstein and Woodward helped bring down a president through their journalism and I found writing to come as easy as public speaking did years later when I'd argue more than a hundred jury trials as a public defender in Philadelphia.

One of my favorite jobs was serving as a union organizer for The Newspaper Guild and then going to law school to become a labor lawyer. I got a D+ in a labor law class and found my true calling defending those accused of crimes over a 20-year career.

The Vietnam War had a lasting effect on me. Post-Traumatic Stress Disorder hit me some 25 years after the war and I ended up seeking help through daily meditation and a spiritual journey I was "forced into" at a young retirement age. It was then that I began to write of my life and how the kid from Brewerytown made his living in a world not often as kind and compassionate as he hoped he would find in growing up.

It was a real roller-coaster ride that I offered piece-meal in Blog posts at WordPress.com. I began writing the posts a year after my retirement. I put them altogether for your perusal and hope that you can identify with some and perhaps feel compassion for ones you are glad you never have had to face in your life.

I tried to be as authentic as possible. Please forgive me ahead of time if you found anything offensive. It is not my intent to hurt anyone but to help others reach a bit of happiness in this lifetime.

Please enjoy the stories here.

Remember what the Buddha taught about how one should view life.

Nothing exists in and of itself.

All things are contingent on other things. In other words, all things are interdependent. I wouldn't be who I am today if it were not for so many people and events that appeared in my life, for those hundreds of causes and conditions that seemed to ripen in and around me as I made choices that lead to so many of life's different paths.

The other thought I have is attributed to my favorite philosopher, Socrates. "An unexamined life if not worth living." I believe that Socrates – or the vision of him that appeared to me in a dream — spoke about writing shortly after I had retired. I saw him in a dream and then worked with his philosophical "ideals" through what Carl G. Jung, the eminent psychologist, called "active imaginations."

I began to write a Blog for WordPress at the time and it has continued through this very moment. Most of what you see here comes directly from the more than 800 "posts" or entries for the blog.

Dedicated to Jameson Alexander Contos

Table of Contents

I The kid's early years

Name-calling can get you kicked in the end

PATTY DEMARCO MADE ME CRY. He called me names and wouldn't stop as I tried to walk away, with him following me on the street in North Philadelphia where we lived. On and on he went, badmouthing me, until he saw my brother, who helped me into his little red wagon, and pulled it home, me sobbing all the while behind. I was four.

"*Refugee*," was one of the names Patty called out to me. "*Deportee*," was another. I didn't know what either meant, but he aimed the words at me and my family. I knew inside they were unkind words. Meant to hurt someone. To make fun of 'em. To belittle 'em.

My father spoke with an accent. He was 15 when he came from Greece, the eldest of nine boys and girls, while making his way in the "*foreign*" land called America during the "*Roaring 20s*." He came from a small fishing village on the Island of Nysiros, a volcanic land mass split into four tiny villages. My dad's homeland had no electricity until the 1960s.

Patty made fun of the way my father talked. Patty also poked fun at the woman across the street that spoke with a German accent. He always said it in a way to make people feel bad. I felt bad for 'em, as well as myself.

As I grew older, I heard other remarks, and while none made me cry, they hurt the same way. "*Spic.*" "*Greeseball.*" And then the variation of the "*N*" word, as in "*n—— – lover,*" against me, and the full ugly word against my friends who happened to be black.

Kids did not come up with those words by themselves. They heard them from their parents. Used at the dinner table by mostly poor white men who were just passing on bigotry from their fathers, and possibly from the oldest one they called grandfather.

And, it probably wasn't just the men. I dated a girl who let her bias show. We had argued and broke up. She called me a "*Spic.*" I thought you had to be Spanish before someone could call you that. This Irish girl knew next to nothing about the world, but learned enough to call someone a name, whether it fit or not.

Some called me a "*little Jew bastard.*" They had gotten my heritage and what I thought was my legitimate birth status completely wrong, but it didn't seem to matter — it fed the fear and ugliness inside of them. Their little minds, their petty need to feel superior by putting down as inferior someone different from themselves.

(See Part II next)

Name-caller gets his butt kicked in the end

Calling a kid names could cause a lasting scar one may have to deal with later in life. It's either that, or you learn to "toughen up" as I did, and let the wise-cracks, the slurs, the hate-filled and ignorant remarks simply glide over you.

I REMEMBER MY TEENAGE YEARS, and names aimed at me by people I didn't know or hardly knew. On occasion, I'd hear somebody call me "*queer.*" I'm not homosexual, *not that there's anything wrong with it*, to quote the old Seinfeld routine. But I never shied away from such "*feminine*" activities as dancing and singing, getting "*dressed up,*" for a party, and "*speaking in complete sentences*" and not the monosyllables used by a lot of so-called "*tough*" guys on the block of North Philadelphia where I grew up.

Later still, I got hit with such labels as "*racist,*" and then "*sexist.*" Neither fit, but I never stayed around those persons long enough to prove them wrong. They did not know me, and I was maturing enough to know my bending over backwards to show them the opposite would be a waste of time. Theirs' and mine.

When it comes to name-calling, I'm not talking ancient history here. I remember returning from a trip to Greece in late 2008 and hearing a comment from a fellow Vietnam veteran twice my size about my fellow countrymen.

We were riding in an elevator full of veterans and this *Patty DeMarco*-type — a bully — asked me if I enjoyed myself with all the *"Greek men"* in Athens.

"Yeah," I said. *"Including your mama."*

It got a big laugh all around, except for the homophobic name-caller, who turned red in his white face. He was the same one who said his parish priest had to *"clean out"* the church recreational hall when a group of Muslims were permitted to hold a meeting there. The guy's old. Age-wise as well as culturally. He's got white hair and lives alone with his PTSD (post-traumatic stress disorder). Few have anything to do with him. Including his family. When will he ever learn that you just can't elevate yourself, you can't improve your lot by trying to tear down another because of their religion, their politics, their way of life?

I kicked *Patty DeMarco's* ass the next time he called me a name while growing up in Brewerytown. Hit him as hard as I could, shouting *"get up, 'shrimp boats,'"* as he fell to the street, cowering next to marble steps leading to one of the row homes on our block. He held both arms over his face, as snot poured out and onto his clothes. Now it was his turn to bawl. The only name he called then, was for his *"mama."* It felt good, but I would not recommend it for an adult who picked up PTSD during his or her lifetime. Could end up in jail and the name-caller in the morgue.

Sticks and stones may break your bones, but names will never hurt you, is how the saying goes. They may not hurt, but I don't think you ever forget them, either. If you're lucky, you use them to either build character or learn how to forgive from a long distance for harms done you a long time ago.

(See part III next)

'Les We Forget' names called our soldiers

No one's ever called me "*baby-killer*."

I never was "*spit on*" upon returning home to the United States following a year at war in Vietnam, while friends and co-workers I met through the years may have thought it, none have said to my face they believed I was one of those "*crazed Vietnam veterans*."

I'm grateful for this absence in my life, particularly after wondering the other day about all the names people have called me while growing up. I forgot about my military life, the three years I spent first as an enlisted man, and the two as a "*90-day wonder*" Lieutenant in the Army. And of course now, that I am one of the veterans with time on their hands to reflect and ponder life.

I believe the term "*baby-killer*" surfaced after *Lt. William Calley,* an officer serving in my old army division, the 23rd, also known as the "American," led a platoon that decimated Vietnamese families in the Village of My Lai. He was in charge of men who lost their humanity and killed indiscriminately, taking the lives of some 300 people, mostly women and children as well as elderly men, with little or no proof they had anything to do with the killings of GIs days earlier, or the possible "*aiding and abetting*" of the Viet Cong. It's true, some of the 26 men under Lt. Calley's command, *did* kill babies. None were ever convicted of any crimes, save the young officer, who ended his silence in recent years and offered his remorse for the actions of his platoon.

All servicemen seemed to have gotten painted with that broad brush by the media and America's collective consciousness shortly after the publicity of My Lai and its cover-up. No one pointed out what General Sherman said a hundred years earlier. And that is "*War is Hell.*" I might add, that <u>all</u> war is hell. Not only to the warriors, but to their families, as well as to the families of the enemies and the "*enemy*" we were ordered to fight.

When I came back to the States from Vietnam, I landed in Fort Lewis, Washington. No protestors greeted me. No one "*spit*" at me or anywhere near my direction.

And I don't have any personal knowledge of any veterans who faced such behavior from the public. None ever mentioned it in the circles of vets I knew in college and at university. And I never heard it from any of whom I covered as a newspaper reporter, or served as a union representative.

Could it have been one of those "*urban legends*" you hear about, but lacks basis from any evidence? And what about the "*crazed Vietnam veteran*" label? I learned through a PTSD (post-traumatic stress disorder) clinic that it was hyped up by the press and Hollywood by good-intentioned liberals seeking to end the Vietnam War. They were in "*cahoots*" with activist psychiatrists and psychologists, as well as many others in the medical professions, who were against the war and used the term to scare America into ending it. Problem is, the term stayed in the collective consciousness and once again tainted all servicemen, even those that may have served as clerks or cooks in a combat zone, or nowhere near the scene of a battle.

It got so bad, that many veterans refused to add their service record to their resumes, believing it would "*turn off*" potential employers.

A study done in the 70s showed that in most situations when a Vietnam veteran became the subject in the movies or on television, he was generally portrayed as a little "*deranged*" at worst, or a "*loose cannon*" at best. The term PTSD, however, had not yet made it into the mainstream. It wasn't until the early 80s that the bible for mental disorders, the *DSM-Diagnostic and Statistical Manual of Mental Disorders*, first mentioned PTSD and its effects on veterans.

And so I am grateful. They could've called me a lot worse than they did. But, as "*Contoveros*," the "*singer of truth*," and an occasional scrivener here, I hope no one ever calls me "*forgetful*."

(I never lost touch with the kid inside of me and I am lucky to visit him when I write. He's the most pure and authentic part of me. He has courage and isn't afraid of new things even though they sometimes appear out of the great unknown.

I can't bullshit him. He knows the truth and he recognizes it after I put it on paper. The kid knows a good story when he reads one. He often smiles and gives me the thumbs up when he recognizes how authentic the small act of creation has turned out. That's what this offering is all about.)

Feeling sorry for others starts with a child

WHEN I WAS A CHILD, I'd feel sorry for anyone who appeared less fortunate than I. That would include the white-haired elderly stooped over with age, as well as the infirm, a word I didn't learn the meaning of until I was much older myself.

It's hard to describe this feeling; saying you feel "sorry" sounds like "pity," but it's not; at least, not in my case. When seeing a person with an obvious disfigurement, or walking with crutches or being pushed in a wheelchair, an overwhelming feeling of concern would well up inside me. I'd wish I could ease their pain, even if they had no pain; I wanted to help them get over their discomfort somehow.

This feeling came from within. There was something innate about it. I knew it was the right thing to feel when I saw the suffering of others. No one could have taught me this. Oh, my parents shared the Golden Rule with me and my brothers. They told us to be kind to other people and to animals.

But you couldn't teach me to "feel" what I now realize was "compassion" and "empathy." It came naturally for me. I believe it comes naturally for all children; that it's part of our basic good nature to "feel sorry" for others. All of us at some point wanted to help others and ease their pain, even if it was just by offering a smile, saying hello, or asking with loving kindness "Can I help you?"

I'd get so much out of helping someone else. I'd feel good inside, a quiet, happy, silent type of joy. I'd never expect anything in return and I'd feel I was doing exactly what the nuns at Catholic school would later advise me was what the Almighty One wanted all of us to do: to care for each other, particularly, the down-and-out.

And then one day someone older than me admonished me and that I was a fool to feel this way; that I shouldn't give to someone begging on the street because he'd just "drink it up." Another person who I thought was wise said that those who were unfortunate "got what they deserved," and that their illnesses or maladies probably were their own fault because of the way "they" lived — never explaining what was meant by "they." You'd understand that it was that person's way of putting down another because of his race, religion, sexual preference or orientation.

I'd be a sucker to care for them, "smarter" adults would tell me, and the child inside would ask how something that made me feel so good could be so bad. You can't get ahead in life, achieve your goals, or make lots of money by offering loving kindness and compassion to others who are suffering, they said.

"Grow up," they all told me.

And I did, quashing these feelings, and challenging the world with a determination to compete, to get ahead, and to succeed no matter what the cost. I'd get awards; see my name and achievements engraved on wall plaques in halls of higher learning and in business. And I'd make a comfortable living, providing for a future where there'd be few concerns or worries.

Something was missing, however, and it wasn't until I connected with the child inside that I realized what it really was. Giving freely to others *was* and *is* "life." Sharing with those with little or nothing provides me with all that I could ever want. Putting another's needs above my own offers me a joy that I've missed since silently cherishing it while much younger.

Offering love to others is a good way to receive love back, but only if it's done with nothing expected in return.

The child inside me had the right feelings all along, I realized. Now that I know this again, let me make it right for all the years I missed not helping you.

May I help you, please?

It would be my pleasure. Thank you.

> *(A recent study found that the pupils of infants' eyes widened when they saw someone in need—a sign of concern—but their pupils would shrink when they could help that person—or when they saw someone else help, suggesting that they felt better. (Babies as young as four or five months will try to help their mothers pick up something dropped on the floor.) They seem to care primarily for the other person and not themselves. It was calming to see the person's suffering being alleviated, whether or not they were the ones who did it.}*

Home where I grew up still haunts my mind

I GREW UP IN A two-story row house in North Philadelphia in a mixed neighborhood of whites and blacks where we all played in front of the fire-plug and got ice from old ice-trucks that made their way up the tiny one-way street.

I remember the small, concrete-covered back yard where my oldest brother had me pitch him a ball and he hit it with a broken tree branch. The branch cracked and flew toward me barely missing my eye by a fraction of an inch. I still carry the scar and relish the story.

I also remember teaching a kid younger than me how to read on our front steps. He was a black boy named Washington. I didn't know I had made such an impact on him until I bumped into him some 40 years later. I was representing a criminal defendant in court and Washington was a police officer in full uniform. When he started to question my background, I thought I was going to be arrested. Instead, he thanked me for helping him enjoy reading. I felt a karmic touch that day.

It was tough growing up in the 1950's, particularity with bigots living on your block. One kid made me cry when he called me "Displaced Person," a term for many Europeans who were being relocated from their homes following the Nazi occupation. My father came from Greece and the smart-alack kid targeted him with venom. (I kicked the kid's ass eventually. Sometimes you gotta stick up for yourself and get a little respect. My old neighborhood taught me how to do that.)

> Home was where my great uncle resided until his death. He was a mean son-of-a-bitch, always yelling and cursing in a language I did not understand -- Greek. He was called Uncle Mike, but may have just been a distant relative that my father took in from his homeland.

Years later, I learned our house had been occupied by a family who suddenly moved out after seeing the mean old white guy roaming with bushy white hair and a bushy beard roaming the hallways upstairs. He had haunted the house, they claimed. No one lived in it since then.

The building no longer stands on Marston Street near 29th Street and Girard Avenue. It was torn down like so many low-income houses that went up when Brewerytown was a thriving section of Philadelphia before Prohibition. The memories of the old neighborhood and first house I grew up in still haunt me today. But mostly in a nice way, if you know what I mean.

The Ice Man Cometh for Me and for Thee

It was the ice on the truck that beckoned to me when I was five-years-old and playing on Marston Street -- the one-way street near my home in North Philadelphia.

At one time, delivery men hauled large blocks of ice in trucks for you to deposit them in the "ice box,' which was the forerunner of the refrigerator. Ask your grandparents or great-grandparents about them. Every family had one, or they used cold storage areas cut out of the ground or a hill.

As a city boy, I grew up in working class area called Brewerytown, I wanted to be just like the older kids who got chunks of ice from the trucks. They'd hold them for what seems like hours, slurping away at the cool refreshment a nice chunk of ice could offer them on a hot day!

I remember climbing onto the back of a truck that day. Reaching in, I tried to grab some of that cold nourishment, when, to my surprise, I next woke up in a hospital bed miles away where someone told me I was being treated for a concussion.

They told me and my family that the ice truck, which had been stationery with its motor running, started moving forward with a jolt as it pulled away, shifting gears.

I must have fallen backwards, striking my head on the street below where some ambulance attendant found me, placed me in his vehicle, and rushed me to St. Joseph's Hospital near Broad Street and Girard Avenue.

I don't remember anything beside that moment clinging to the back of the truck on little Marston Street. I spoke to no one who would admit they had been with me when I tried such a foolish trick. My parents and their parents would have chewed them out for letting someone as young as I was then do such a crazy thing.

I often wonder today whether my later growth might have been stunted or perhaps altered somehow by the ice-run accident. We're finding out more and more about concussions and their effect on the brain. I recall getting treatment years later for "anger management" and one of the questions raised by psychologists was whether you ever had a concussion or other blows to the head. I readily admitted it, having had my fair share of street fights in the neighborhood. I didn't know the hits to the head would have such lasting effects however.

Maybe that explains why I suffered from PTSD (Post-Traumatic Stress Disorder) years after serving in combat while in Vietnam. I never got hit by any enemy rounds, but I did suffer mentally, and perhaps emotionally, when artillery shells fell near me and around the platoon I had led. You don't know how shattering the noise can be when something built to kill people crashes onto the ground where you are walking or sleeping.

It can have a chilling effect on any one at any age.

Dream of Smith's Playground inspires me

SWINGING FROM ONE TARZAN-LIKE VINE to another can be thrilling to most youngsters.

I remember feeling just like Johnny Weissmuller, the original Tarzan, as I'd dream about the "*monkey swing*" at Smith's Playground in North Philadelphia. Whenever I wanted to achieve something worthwhile in my life. I'd visualize myself swing from one achievement to another, always going forward as I stretched out an arm to grab one metal ring and then the next one on down the line.

It's a daydream I'd call up before falling asleep, seeing myself ascend to a higher realm, one beyond my grasp, but would somehow become visible in my make-believe world. No matter what the goal: attending community college, going to the university, and before too long, a career as a newspaper reporter.

The "*dream of the rings*" surfaced when trying out for the high school gym team. I learned that I had good upper body strength while at Dobbins Technical School at 22nd Street and Lehigh Avenue. It helped me later at basic training as well as Officers' Candidate School where push-ups made you fit right into life in the infantry.

But the rings at the North Philadelphia playground were my actual building blocks. I went there when I was five years old. I'd spend most of my time at the world's largest indoor slide. A slide someone waxed daily to insure a smooth ride over a shiny, heavily lacquered wood.

I remember climbing 30 to 40 steps to get to the top, where three or four kids could safely sit across the crest of the slide, look down below and get ready to push off from the rear.

Glorious feelings took over: exhilaration, excitement, some fear, but mostly a joyousness that still rings clear across the decades. Couldn't hear yourself think for the screams all around you. Reminded me of the screams I'd hear years later from a roller coast ride.

But here, there were no security bars to keep you in place. No person sitting close to hold your hand. You were on your own, a free spirit gliding downward, occasionally noticing the rich smell of polished wood right after a good rain, or the honeysuckle giving off its scent from bushes growing outside.

Too soon, you'd reach the bottom, looking up for your mom or an older sibling watching over you. Took 20 minutes of waiting in line to get the thrill of a lifetime. And one day, after two or three rides, someone introduced me to what I call the "*monkey swing*" rings.

You could only reach the first ring by walking up a slanted wooden platform until you were three feet above the ground. You had to be tall enough to reach the ring that hung from a chain attached to a thick metal pole some 25 feet above. There were six or seven rings all in a row, equally distanced apart.

The object was to swing like a monkey from one ring to another, until you made it to the end, and then return without touching the ground. I don't remember how long it took to finally make such a "round trip." I'd try the rings every chance I'd get. That is, until I noticed callouses developing for the first time. I learned early there were some things in life you had to toughen up and prepare in order to achieve. Building callouses was one of them. It helped me grab the rings better, insurer a stronger grip and give me confidence I lacked before.

I remember what it was like to finally complete the exercise and travel back and forth over the rings. I see it when I close my eyes and want to "*relive*" those moments filled with a stubborn determination to prove I could accomplish it.

It's something that gives me as much pleasure now as it did back then. Without callouses. Without years of trial and error until achieving a little enlightenment.

(See Part II next)

Dream of swinging on a star rings out

Dreaming about Smith's Playground *and the challenges of the rings, I see myself reaching out with my right hand and grabbing the first metal ring.*

I would stand on my toes to pull it closer to the wooden platform I was balanced on. Gotta pull the ring back. Pull it so I can get the proper swing to the next ring. If you glide out without an extra pull, you'd fall short and drop to the ground, a failure.

I DISCOVERED THE ONLY WAY I could to swing correctly was to learn by trial and error. I must have swung out dozens of times to get the proper feel. I watched others and saw how graceful they looked. Like a Tarzan swinging from the vines, the white ape I wanted to emulate. (Did I tell you that *Johnny Weissmuller,* the original Tarzan, may have once lived just a few blocks away from Smith's' Playground in North Philadelphia, where I was a child at play? A barber my father took me to on Columbia Avenue swore that Weissmuller lived there!)

There's something about swinging that would make me feel in charge. — feel in control. Like I'm a master — a leader of all my thoughts, energies and physical movements.

There's nothing like absorbing the air breeze through your hair, feel the coolness on your face, the ears and the tips of your nose and lips. Reminds me of what it might be like jumping out of an airplane as a bona-fide paratrooper in the Army's elite Airborne School. To feel so alone, yet so much in unity — like one with the universe — when you make that first "jump" into the air.

There, I made it to the second ring and now the momentum is carrying me forward. No time to think of what to do next. Simply do it! Reach out and grab the third ring and glide forward. Onto the next one and the next, until you reach the end and turn around to head back.

Have to remember to pace myself, not to "*over swing*" and get tired on reaching the end ring. I failed by trying too hard, pushing myself when I should have saved energy for the long haul. Confidence growing, I'd reach out, feeling my way back. I have actually seen myself accomplishing this task long before physically achieving it. Some will call this "*visualization*." I did it as a kid. Is it something I sensed? Something I knew how to do from some innate knowledge?

The last ring was just ahead, I seemed to recall. It seems so easy now. But, it took so long to reach. There were times I wanted to give up; I didn't believe I'd be good enough, strong enough, or even brave enough to see it through to the end. And there I was.

Mission accomplished. Goal achieved. Finish line finally reached!

Funny. I thought I'd feel more triumphant. Like there should be crowds cheering me on like I'm a Caesar riding through the streets of a loud, boisterous Roman city.

Oh, I enjoyed the accomplishment. It was a thrill to finally make it. I'd feel great, and I think it helped ensure my future well-being. I felt I could do anything I set my mind to. But in some ways, I'd also feel it marked the start of a long process, like it was just the beginning of placing notches along a line of other achievements, other goals and even detrimental experiences that someone would dare me to try someday.

I wouldn't trade this for anything in the world. I only wished I could have taken more time to cherish this, to enjoy it while it was going on instead of gazing over the horizon to the next challenge.

I learned that that I needed to spend more time being in the *moment.* To Love the one moment I was in.

Like . . . *right now.*

Touched by an Angel to Help Guide Others

Angels can perform magic if we open ourselves to 'em!

Today while in what I call the "post-meditative-state," I wondered if something spiritual might have occurred when I was much younger. I then thought of a time when I was in first grade in Saint Ludwig's Roman Catholic Church School. Sister St. Leonard had chosen me to be one of her so-called "angels." The duty of an "angel" was to guide the second graders to the front of the church where they were to receive their first Holy Communion by a priest. I remember I was standing at the end of a pew where the second graders had been kneeling during a church service. I was wearing pure white. I had on white shoes, white pants, white shirt and a white cape that had a blue silk lining. Looking back, I know that I must have appeared quite dashing! There is a picture taken by a family member showing me in the angel outfit standing outside of Saint Ludwig's Church. I look quite angelic in my get up. I'm in front of a column carved into one of the church's entrance way.

On reflection about my earliest encounter with the spiritual world, I couldn't help but wonder if there was some sort of reason that I was called to serve others in the House of the Creator. Maybe it was a first calling of sorts.

There must have been something in me that one of my least favorite nuns saw that I couldn't see. There must have been something good that kind of stuck out or showed in what I later learned could have been my aura of sort.

I believed in Jesus. I believed that whenever I did something bad or sinful, it hurt Jesus. The worst thing in the world to a kid of that age, I believe, was to do something intentionally negative, be it an act or thought, or even a thought or act of omission. I believed it made Jesus weep.

Maybe that is what Sister St. Leonard had seen in me back then. Maybe it was one of the angels who surrounded me as a child, manifesting for the nun to see the entity.

I like to think there were other times when the divine engulfed me so much that I couldn't do anything except the Will of God. Hey, that ain't so bad, come to think of it. It's kind of like being touched by an angel to help humanity see and feel the unconditional love in the universe. Who needs to be a medium when you can be a mystic?

Art helps this kid appreciate all of his life!

ONE OF MY PLAYGROUNDS WHEN I was growing up was the Philadelphia Museum of Art in the Fairmount section of the City of Brotherly Love.

I lived in a neighborhood called Brewerytown located just north of the museum. I'd walk eight blocks and climb on the rocks that surround much of the grounds. There was something challenging about reaching out to the boulder just above my head while I pulled myself up and onto the next rocks. I didn't need playmates. I became a solitary mountain climber about to scale a Mount Everest of my mind.

I'd also play in the shallow pools toward the front of the museum. The steps are familiar to most people who saw the movie "Rocky." Hidden off the side of the steps are concrete pools of water no deeper than a foot or two. I usually played with other fellows from the old neighborhood and had a ball looking toward the east where the statue of William Penn, the founder of Pennsylvania, rested on top of city hall where I would try jury trials many years later.

I'd go into the museum proper every now and then. We got in free on Sundays.

What greeted you upon entering was this giant statue of a warrior, a tall metal one at the top of the steps. It was a girl -- Diana, the huntress from the age of the Romans. Her Greek name was Artemis. I didn't know that women were ever depicted as soldiers or warriors and the statue opened my eyes to a world I had never imagined before.

So did this really gross picture, a painting of a guy in the nude trapped on the side of a mountain by Peter Paul Rubens. A large black eagle is depicted chewing a red, slimy part of his body -- the liver -- ripping it from his uncovered side. The fellow was one my father's countrymen, a Greek, who pissed off the gods by steeling fire from Olympus and sharing it with the rest of mankind. The old Greek gods doomed Prometheus to be forever chained to the mountain with the bird feasting on him for all of eternity.

One of my favorite recollections from the museum was the large painting by the French Impressionist Pierre-Auguste Renoir. He painted a bunch of women near a stream and he entitled it *"The Bathers."* The attractive women had different hair colors, but all shared the same type of physical attributes. They were large women and girls. Bountiful is the word I learned from seeing that painting. I fell I love with them and see how attractive Renoir made what most women actually look like. They became part of my playground and the appreciation of true beauty ever since.

Confession of a Kresge juvenile delinquent

TODAY WE HAVE THE DOLLAR Store but when I was growing up we kids enjoyed the Five and Dime Store.

Believe it or not, there were semi-department stores like the SS Kresge store that offered odds and ends for very low prices. You could buy lots of stuff for a nickel or a ten cents. I was always saw shopping there as an adventure. We're talking about the Eisenhower years. That's President Eisenhower to those born after the Age of Clinton.

I got caught shoplifting at one of the stores. It was along the main street of Brewerytown, with stores along Girard Avenue in North Philadelphia. Stephen Girard was the name of the philanthropist that opened a school for orphaned boys. Years later, progressives got a court to change his will and allow African American boys attend there. But that was long after I got caught at the Kresge store near 28th Street.

I really didn't want any of the things I grabbed. It was more of the thrill I guess. A really tall woman caught me and scared the crap out of me when she stopped me in one of aisles. I remember as if it was only yesterday. She asked me what school I went to and who my teacher was. I confessed and told her of the Catholic school — St Ludwig's — two blocks away. "Sister Josephine Francis," was the teacher's name I offered while gazing at the wooden floor unable to look the lady in the eye.

"What would the good nun say about you if she knew you were taking things that didn't belong to you?" She asked. I never answered her and felt the worse shame I have ever experienced.

Dollar stores will soon fade away, just like the old Five-and-Ten-Cent Stores. Now there's a place called "Five Below" which makes you think a five-dollar bill is nothing but small change.

But somethings will never change. Lessons learned the hard way through shame and guilt are some of them. Confessing your sins are another. Maybe I can get some good merit at a place I hear called the Million-Dollar-Heaven for my efforts in confessing this crime. It would be well worth the cost to finally admit I was wrong.

Serving graciously as a St. Ludwig altar boy

"Ad Deum Qui Laetificat Juventutem Meam!" – *Latin**

THAT'S ONE OF THE PRAYERS I would recite as an altar boy at St. Ludwig's Roman Catholic Church and I'll never forget it 'til the day I die. Don't ask me what it means. I never figured it out, but I loved to say it!

It was fun serving as an altar boy. I'd get up much earlier than the rest of my family. (Well, my mom would make sure I got up . . .) I'd dress while it was still dark outside. For some reason, I'd always get assigned the early mass just as the Daylight Savings Time switched back to the earlier time of the year!)

I loved getting dressed in the cassock and surplus. The cassock of course was the long black gown that buttoned up in the front. It was just like the one the priest wore. Then I covered my top with the white surplus and "Walla!!" I'd be transformed from the budding juvenile delinquent to the budding holy man.

Funerals were tough to serve. You'd always be teamed up with a friend and you couldn't help but giggle and laugh at the most somber of moments during the funeral mass. I would fight to keep a smile off of my face, but one of the hardest things to do as a kid was not to act up and laugh sometimes when you were in church. When a friend of your own age is doing it, it becomes contagious.

Anyone remember Forty Hours?

Well, that was the period of time the priests would remove the Eucharist from the little house on the altar and display it outside of its home. For 40 hours, we altar boys would stand watch over it – actually, we would kneel -- just to protect it from any non-believers or heathens bent on destruction of the Faith. I always admired the priest when he'd show up and then prostrate himself on the hard marble floor of the church in honor of the Host. I wish I could be as humble in all of my dealings in life.

I experienced my first Touch of the Divine as an altar boy. Yeah, I had met a 12-year-old girl the night before and I went to church and prayed on a kneeler for her love. (I actually prayed that she would "like" me. I didn't know that much about love at that age. I was 12 myself.)

All of a sudden I felt transformed into another realm, one that I would experience dozens of years later when meditating and tasting the bliss of whatever you want to call that divine intervention.

I felt the Presence of God. Nothing could go wrong. I was totally loved and would always be loved no matter what might happen or who might come into my path.

I was love. And love was me.

> The little altar boy at St. Ludwig's Roman Catholic Church in a section of Philadelphia called Brewerytown. What I wouldn't give to return to those moments of innocence and divine feelings. What's that you say? I can do it anytime I want to by simply closing my eyes and remembering the Latin prayers and my bell-ringing days?

Yeah, just like now. Recollect and reflect Michael J. I'll say a little prayer for you but this time I might say in in Sanskrit. I don't think you'll feel any different because it deals with the same Source.

(*"*Ad Deum Qui Laetificat Juventutem Meam!*" -- **To God, Who gives joy to my youth**.)

City Differences Create a Variety in My Life

I'D GIVE ANYTHING TO TASTE the flavor of a cherry-chocolate soda.

Not the ones from a bottle. A soda fountain drink! Nothing compares to the delicious mixture of "*real*" chocolate and cherry syrups combined with that seltzer-like substance that produced a drink that could have originated only in Paradise.

And, it just wasn't the soda! It was the anticipation as you played with the nickel or dime in your hand, an 8-year-old who snuck away from the front of the house and made his way down the block and around the corner to the pharmacy that stood at 28th and Master streets in Brewerytown, North Philadelphia.

Kaplan's Pharmacy, with its metal padded stools you could twist and twirl to your heart's content after placing an order for your favorite beverage. I could barely climb onto the chair without help, but once perched on it, I'd pretend I was much older, say 10 or 11, in hopes that Mrs. Kaplan would not ask too many questions about my mom or my older brothers. She knew the family. That's the way it was in the old neighborhood. The proprietors would see you together so often, they became your extended family, offering genuine care and consideration when they could.

Mrs. Kaplan was one of several Jewish store-keepers in my limited world at that age. I wasn't allowed to cross a major street and had to confine myself to the one square block bordered by 28th and 27th on the east-west directions and Master and Jefferson streets on the north-south.

In addition to Kaplan's, there were two *"candy"* stores — Barr's and Fischer's. We also had a traditional *"mom and pop"* store on our tiny block of Marston Street. It was Kramer's, which served up sandwich meats and rolls, as well as milk and eggs when we ran out of food purchased from the supermarket. We'd spend a lot of time at Kramer's because neither my father nor mother owned or drove a car. The nearest supermarket was at 26th and Girard Avenue, about six blocks away.

Two blocks from home on Thompson Street is where Klein's Pharmacy and "Sy's Steak Shop" offered their goods. (Sy's, by the way, was one of the homes of the original Philly cheese steaks.) Jewish families ran each of the businesses mentioned.

Today, Asians own many of the same properties, serving the old neighborhood of mostly African-Americans and immigrants trying to grab onto the American dream to become upwardly mobile.

Greeks and people from India shared that dream, and found pathways in the restaurant and modern convenience stores. There is a lot of truth in the old joke of two Greeks meeting in a town for the first time. *One of them will always open a restaurant!* I'd say there is a higher plurality of folks from India operating and working in 7-11 and other convenience stores than most other minority groups. Same with Greeks at restaurants.

That's one of the reasons I like my all-time favorite drink. I'm drawn to these kind of *"unusual"* things. The same with the people and places I visit. They offer familiarity and give a sense of order. Eating pizza out of a Greek joint; listening to the Indian fellow's accent at the Wawa convenience store; seeing *"Chinese"* stores run by Asians of all backgrounds provide a variety of foods in the inner cities.

I guess that's what makes growing up in a city extra special. You develop a hankering for all kinds of unique, individual and different tastes. Prepares you for accepting more out of life than you could have imagined by yourself.

Like a cherry-chocolate soda made by that wonderfully nice Jewish lady, Mrs. Kaplan.

Al Brown taught 8-yr-old lesson of lifetime

I ALWAYS LOOKED UP TO Al Brown. Nowadays, I guess you would call him a *"community organizer,"* someone in the neighborhood a person could turn to with questions about the block, the new and older people who lived on your street. Like that section of Brewerytown where I grew up in North Philadelphia.

He must have had some *"connections."* Not at any high level, but for small things like, turning on a fireplug during the hottest days of the summer. Al Brown had one of those specialized wrenches, the ones owned primarily by firefighters who used them to turn on a hydrant for battling a fire.

The hydrant on the 1400 block of Marston Street was just north of middle of the one way street. Those with cars parked on the one side, seemed to always be home when the hydrant was *"opened,"* and graciously moved their vehicles, thus allowing a dozen or more kids to splash unimpeded the entire length of the narrow street.

Motorists would cooperate. Slow to a crawl, while rolling up their windows to prevent us more advanced hydrant *"operators"* to splash their cars as they drove by.

You could cause the water to spray if you sat behind the fire plug, legs stretched in front and around the hydrant base, while leaning into the center of the plug, wrapping both arms around the front, and clasping your hands together, with fingers interlaced. Pulling your hands over the gushing water, you could make the liquid shoot into the air, creating an arc of water as kids younger than yourself (and sometimes their parents), would run "*inside*" the arc, remaining dry until spotted by the hydrant "*shooter.*"

I could always tell when a person was trying hard to avoid wetting their hair. It was usually an "*older*" teenage girl or a young mom. I'd show them no mercy.

"*Gotcha*" I'd cry out as I maneuvered the water into their direction, hoping the stream of water would hit their head as they turned and screamed when getting the full blast. The kid in them came out as soon as they realized how much fun they could have wet all over.

Smaller kids would simply lie in the gutter of the street, letting the water rush over them as they made "*snow angels*" on the black macadam, letting the water form "*ponds*" as it flowed into the outstretched legs and groin area. We'd advise smaller kids not to swallow any of the water. Even at the mid-point of the 20th century we had concerns about Philadelphia's water supply, especially the one provided for emergencies.

Al Brown also worked at the Fairmount Movie Theater, once at 26th and Girard Avenue, directly across from Girard College for Boys.

He'd open the side door when he recognized the kids from his block. Let us "*sneak*" in during a matinee and save the cost of admission — I believe it was a whole quarter! He'd wink at you, like a conspirator, and tell you not to say anything. And I never did. Until now.

Al Brown may have been my first honest-to-Goodness role model. He was athletic, wise, smart and "*savvy.*" Could also be sensitive and protect the smaller ones against bullies of all shapes, sizes and colors. I wanted to be just like him.

Al Brown was black. An African-American who showed kids like me to be "*color blind*" and to accept all people as authentic, and to befriend those who had something we called "*heart*."

He taught me lessons at age 8 that I have never forgot. Thanks Al Brown. *You* had a lot of heart. See you in the next life.

'I confess!' I cut school with Franny O

I'M GOING TO CONFESS. I played hooky in seventh grade and refused to *"squeal"* on the kid I stayed out of class with that day.

I never talked, even when Sister St. Clare, a real penguin of a Catholic nun, backed me up to a metal stairway, finger-pointing accusingly on my chest, forcing me to take a step backwards where I fell the entire length of the stairs, surviving with nary a broken bone, or a broken spirit.

I refused to name names even when the nun summoned one of the big guns, a priest serving as assistant pastor who took no further action against me, and actually admired my *chutzpah* for protecting someone I felt I could not betray.

The culprit was Franny O. The skinny kid who had a retort for everything. The only real *"certified"* juvenile delinquent I knew growing up in Brewerytown, a tough, working class section of North Philadelphia.

Franny *"influenced"* me — the wrong way. The *"bad"* way, if you want to know the truth. He smoked cigarettes, cursed using the "F" word, and had no respect for religion or those in authority.

I wanted to be just like him!

He had charisma. A good-looking kid, with a swagger about himself, like a young James Cagney, if you remember the old gangster movies. Cagney was short. Under 5′ 8." I identified with him. And with Franny.

Don't know much of Franny's background. Came from what we called a "*broken*" home, one where a divorce can shatter the integrity of a family. You can say all you want about how bad a fractured, "*dysfunctional*" family is, one where mother and father simply stay together for the sake of the kids. But, at least it is a family. It's intact and if there's no abuse, I think kids have a better chance of reaching their full potential, whatever one later deems that to be.

I went to the city dump with Franny. Had never been there before. Snow covered the ground. Got tired of our little "*adventure*" in less than an hour of nosing around junk and smelly odds and ends. We ran off when we spotted a police officer. Couldn't wait to get out of the cold and to go home, where I snuck into the basement, and hid on a shelf in a built-in closet. It took forever for noon to arrive, when I got out, went outside, and entered the front door, pretending I just came from school for lunch.

Damn it! I misplaced my book bag. Mom had gotten me one of those with a handle and imitation leather, like I was some miniature lawyer going to the office. Got to remember where I left it . . . (Got caught when the police found it. They called my mother and the school, where a sadistic nun took it as a *sign* to beat the living daylights out of me. My fall down the steps actually helped save me.)

Franny O "*did time*" at St. Gabriel's Home for Boys outside Philadelphia. It was what was called a "*reform school*" for kids the legal profession termed "*incorrigible*." Taken out of his residence, he roomed with dozens of others in his age group, where he could either learn to follow society's rules, or hone a craft outside the rules.

Franny's appeal took a hit, and he lost a little of my respect when he was "*disciplined*" by one of the nuns in a classroom at St. Ludwig's Catholic School. Not sure what infraction he committed, but the black-robed sister smacked him repeatedly across his butt, as Franny yelled and kept placing his hands behind him to ward off the assaults of a wooden pointer. He cursed. That only made things worse, as the roomful of kids sat and watched the beating. Our teacher broke the thick pointer on his rear end. He should have taken the punishment "*like a man,*" I thought. Instead, Franny cried, showing he was no stronger than the rest of us at such a tender age.

Had not seen Franny for years, until bumping into him at the "*T & B*" bar at Taney and Browns streets, in Fairmount a dozen or more years later. He worked there as a bartender. I had been drafted into the army and on my way to being commissioned a second lieutenant. Hardly recognized Franny. We had nothing to say, having both gone in different directions by then.

I saw him again nearly 20 years later. He was in Philadelphia Common Pleas Court. No, not a defendant, but a citizen bringing a private criminal complaint against a neighbor. I was a young lawyer, and tried to tell Franny the little I learned about the Judge and the system. But, he refused any and all advice. Same old Franny. He'll do things his way. Learn by getting hit upside the head. Or some other spot.

A few years ago while meditating with a Zen Buddhist group, I heard that Franny died. Jack P, a retired police officer, told me about the death when I had visited the old neighborhood. We exchanged stories about Franny – including the ones above -- and had nothing but praise for Theresa C, the girl who married Franny, and possibly provided some of the better things in life for him.

Hope Franny doesn't mind that I've "*dropped the dime*" on him all of these years later.

I didn't think it would come to any harm after all of these years.

Franny O, we hardly knew you. May you rest in peace!

Growing up with Catholic Sisters (Nuns)!

WHILE GROWING UP IN A Catholic School, I met all kinds of nuns. Some I liked more than others. I was kind of like the class clown, or a class-clown wannabe, and got called out by many of the good teachers wearing the black coverings with the bullet-proof white vests covering their chests. I went to Saint Ludwig's, a church school in what was then a predominantly German neighborhood of North Philadelphia called *"Brewerytown."*

I never did like Sister Saint Clare, and I kinda shied away from Sister St. Leonard, due in part for what she did to one of my brothers. He was chewing gum or breaking some dumb rule and got caught. So she made him sit in the waste can in the front of the classroom. When he refused to go to school for several days because of the humiliating experience, she had made him repeat first grade and was forever marked in God's permanent record as one of those who were "left-behind."

Sister Saint Clare bullied me when she learned I had played hooky. She tried to get me to "squeal" on who I had stayed out of school with. But I never snitched on him, even after she forced me to the brink of the top of the second floor school stairway and over the steps for a tumble I will never forget.

Sister Josephine Francis was my all-time favorite, even though she smacked me once when I thought it wasn't right. She had left the classroom and told us kids not to talk. It was the type of instruction that hardly anyone followed. At least I didn't, even though I noticed that some kids actually read their books.

When she returned to the room, she asked which one of us had talked. I was unafraid. Like I said, I really liked her. She made me proud of my Greek heritage when she taught us in her fourth grade class about the ancient Greeks, and how much our western world owed to those great men and women from thousands of years ago. I saw myself as one of those who, incidentally, would never tell a lie.

I was one of only a handful — all boys, I seem to recall — who raised our hands in answer to the good sister's questions. Well, without further ado, she marched up to each and everyone one of us sitting in one of those wooden chairs with those little wooden desks with an empty hole across the desk-top that once held an ink bottle, and smacked us.

I mean "smacked" us. It was loud. And, it hurt! But not as much as what happened next.

Pure unadulterated shame and embarrassment came over me. For the first time in my life, I felt my face turning red. You see, I had sinned and the Angel of the Lord descended upon me and struck me with the wrath of God.

It was devastating. Yet, some 50-odd years later, I still hold that holy nun in the highest regard, and I've never been afraid of admitting my mistakes. I could have gone the other way. I could have become someone who would lie by simply saying nothing, which I believe many others might have done. And some still do . . .

Truth is the truth no matter what age you're confronted with it, I learned back then. I feel Sister Josephine Francis helped me to see that and pass a test of a lifetime.

(I feel fortunate to have experienced something far greater in my life when I was a youngster. I didn't know what spiritual stuff was all about when I was young. The full impact of a spiritual life didn't hit me until I retired and had time to think deep philosophical thoughts and to follow different paths.

Looking back, I saw how the divine touched me in so many ways even though I couldn't put my finger on it then and tell you what was happening. That's the great thing about reflection and writing down what one remembers in their life. You get to see and feel thigs differently. You get to appreciate how you were never quite alone as a kid and that someone or something was always looking out for you and guiding you if you simply opened yourself to that possibility. That is a mystical experience I enjoyed while seeking the love of a girl before I had even become a teenager.

Check out the following posts written years apart from each other)

Sharing a little mysticism from days of old

I EXPERIENCED THE PRESENCE OF God when I was 12 years old but didn't know it until some fifty years later when I meditated and realized how much the Divine had filled me when praying for a girl I had just met on that glorious pre-teenage weekend.

I was smitten by Geraldine McFadden, a 12-year-old who lived at Second Street and Allegheny in North Philadelphia. We kissed ever so gently at first and before I knew it, she showed me what it was like to kiss as an adult. In other words, she taught me how to "French Kiss."

I wanted nothing more in life than for her to like me, I mean "**really like me**." And so early Sunday morning I went to church. It was St. Ludwig's Roman Catholic Church in a section called Brewerytown and I dressed up as an altar boy with a black cassock and a white surplus. I went to the kneeler in the Sacristy and I knelt and closed my eyes, envisioning what it was like on the night I had met this heart throb. I began to pray that she would feel the same way toward me as I did toward her.

I prayed and I prayed and then something that has never happened to me occurred.

I went into some sort of a trance. Looking back, I believe it was a meditative state of mind where all thoughts are diminished and you obtain a clear sight into the place of "Nothing" that I read years later that mystics often tap into.

I experienced a joy I had never felt before. Peace and calm descended on me and I had no worries, no thoughts of any past sins and I enjoyed myself being alive in the here and the now. I felt unconditional love from the Universe and Geraldine McFadden didn't seem to matter to me as much anymore.

What I experienced was the Presence of God, but I didn't realize it until some eight years ago when I began to write a Blog and I started to remember some of the events of my life. In *A Course of Love,* we're "taught" to remember who we were in the past. To remember who our true self was and to see life in a way we might have never looked because of the "busy-ness," the stress of work, and the mundane trials and tribulations of daily life.

I was fearful of sharing this with those I grew up with in the working class neighborhood I was raised. I felt *vulnerable* and I thought they'd ridicule or make fun of me as someone "different" and too weird to be accepted by them. I still feel that way sometimes. At least the kid in me feels that, the little "Mikey Contos" inside who is a still sensitive despite his bluster and creds from street fighting and later as an infantry platoon leader in the war of his generation.

I am grateful that I can share my mystical experience without worrying what my old friends and school mates would think of me. They might have had similar experiences and are only now feeling comfortable to share it with others. I want them to know that I am listening and will enjoy their story no matter how crazy they think it might sound. Being present for the Presence of the Higher Self is all that matters.

Love's First Kiss Lasts . . . For Ever More

FIRST KISS? I CAN'T REMEMBER. Must have been a "*forgettable*" one.

First "*French*" kiss? Now, you're talking. I was 12. It was at a party in the cellar of the home of Claire Rober, a girl from my old neighborhood. We played a version of post office and whispered messages to each other along a line until they got mangled up by the time they reached the last person. We were all innocent and had a lot of innocent fun.

And then lights were turned down low, and people paired up. An older girl was with a fellow and most of us laughed when we heard her say in a stage whisper "*that's my girdle.*" I didn't pay much mind. You see, I ended up with the "new" girl, a gymnast visiting Claire from outside the neighborhood, the love of my young life. *Geraldine McFadden.*

Gerry was short and compact. She was athletic and wore one of those clinging gym outfits. Short brunette, with brown eyes that seem to sparkle and say "*smile*" each time she looked at you. "*She flipped over me,*" is the story I told later about my first ever meeting with her.

She performed a gymnastic flip when I asked Claire if her friend could show us one of her moves. She did . . . right in the upstairs dining room of the small row home in Brewerytown, a working class neighborhood of North

Philadelphia. *"Be careful."* some adult told Geraldine as she hit the carpeted floor and shook the keepsakes in the China closet.

I loved her immediately. But who knew if it was reciprocal? Yet somehow I ended up with her in the basement later. But I had heard that Jimmy Suss, two years my senior and a fellow I always looked up to, had his eye on Gerry and made some moves on her. Jimmy was cool. If she liked him more than me, well, no hard feelings. He could have her. You know what I mean?

But, there we were, two kids seated next to one another. About 20 other youngsters somewhere else in the old concrete cellar. This was before the days of the *"rec room."* I'm talking concrete floors, white *"chalky-like"* brick walls, and skinny wooden beams across the ceiling providing support and not any form of decoration.

(See Part II next)

First Love Found, Never Lost a Heart Beat

What was it like to be pre-teen, meeting a person who'd, maybe one day, be the true love of your life? And what did you do when someone turned down the lights in the cellar party . . . and you were alone . . . finally. Your hands touched, your eyes melted while looking at the other's face, their smile, their warm and inviting eyes.

GERALDINE MCFADDEN AND I KISSED. Very shyly. We said few words, none of which I remember now. I tried to make her laugh. She did! And oh, how my heart filled up. {She likes me, at least a little, I thought} I don't know who moved closer to the other. Maybe it was mutual. But soon we were looking eye to eye, more intently, wanting to take in and remember the magic of the moment. I closed my eyes involuntarily. (Was this a reflex move or an action I carried over from a previous life?) I moved my head closer. And she moved her head. We kissed a second time, but this time with a lot more feeling, a lot more . . . love. Puppy Love.

"Do you know how to 'French' kiss," she asked, almost in a whisper. *"I'm not sure,"* I lied, not wanting to show my lack of manly knowledge. I mean, c'mon. You had an image to keep up, even at age 12, going on 13 (actually, turning 13 in a few short weeks back then).

Geraldine explained the technique to me. And we experimented. What an eye-opener! Well, lip-opener really. *"Just open a little,"* she softly said to me, and I complied. What she didn't tell me, and what I learned by *"word of mouth"* was what to do with that small appendage that often got me into trouble from wagging it too much: my tongue.

I swear I did not know what she was doing. I had opened my lips and felt a soft, almost liquid push against first the bottom and then the top lip. Exciting can't describe that first feeling. Try electrifying. Another person, a gorgeous girl who I just met and fell head over heels in love with, had extended the softest part of her body to me in an exchange of trust, love and . . . wait a minute! This ain't kids' stuff I'm dealing with here. This is the real thing, this could be the start of S E X.

I don't like to admit it, I don't think most guys would, but up until that moment in life, I never thought of a real life girl as a potential mate. Oh, I liked girls. But in a shy, bashful way. I liked being with them, liked seeing them smile in my direction, and liked to hear them laugh.

But what do you do with them once you get to first base? I felt I had never been up to bat, and here I am, already being walked by a pitcher who is giving me a *"pass"* to try for second! I'll never forget that kiss. My tongue darted out and made contact with Geraldine's lips and then . . . we . . . *"soul kissed."*

God, I have not thought of that term in ages. *Soul Kiss*. That is so *"right"* for a description. Particularly, when applied to two novices, two youngsters exploring, making their way through adolescence with the help of, and through the trust of, each other.

I cherish that kiss even now as one of the highlights of my life. But there were two other major episodes that had occurred the weekend I met Geraldine McFadden. Each compete for the fondest memory of my life. And all occurred on one fabulous weekend.

Come visit some more, have a little red wine, and I'll tell you about them. But not today. Let me soak in the warmth of this moment a little while longer. Here's to Geraldine and that young rascal, Michael J!

(See Part III next)

Youth recaptured through football hurdle

You can recapture your youth by simply recalling a time in your life when you were your most athletically gifted and soared like an eagle in whatever endeavor you excelled at years earlier.

All you have to do is to focus on an event, one in which you were the center of attention, and recall it in as much detail as possible. Something takes place through your memory recall, your body chemistry, that recaptures the feeling you had then — you re-live the emotions you experienced — and you can stretch out that feeling for as long as you can sustain it. You will become that energetic, gifted young person once again by simply envisioning your shining moment.*

My life's highlight came when I was 12 years old. I was a small, tough kid from a working class neighborhood. I played "*sandlot*" football and was picked to be one of the kick-off return players for a group of teens in a section of North Philadelphia called Brewerytown, a blue-collar mix of mostly Germans, Irish and Poles, with a growing minority of African-Americans. My family was the only Greeks.

Kids from the more "*affluent*" adjoining neighborhood, Fairmount, had challenged us to a football game. The older guys decided to play it on the field near Lemon Hill, walking distance from the Philadelphia Art Museum made famous when Sylvester Stallone ran up the steps as "*Rocky.*"

I didn't know it, but I was the youngest on either sides. I was also reckless, and had just begun to forge a reputation for having a *"lot of heart,"* and for being able to *"take a punch."* I could take pain without complaining, and never, ever *"rat out* "a friend who played hooky from school, snuck in a downtown movie theater, or stole packs of cigarettes from the corner grocer when an order sent the owner into the rear of the store and one need only to lean a certain way to snatch a pack or two from the nearby counter.

Two of the *"old heads,"* the older teens among us, wore their high school football equipment, with shoulder pads, cleats, and padded running pants. One played for each side. The rest of us played in regular street clothes. Guess who were the only two that got injured that day? You got it. The uniformed guys. One was JoJo Guiliano who lived a block away and limped back to his home on Ogden Street.

It was a brisk fall afternoon that day. Leaves had just begun to fall and lay scattered on the grasslands of Fairmount Park, the largest park totally within a municipality in the world. Sun shined through the oak trees that lined the parkway and the streets veering away from the old Philadelphia waterworks and the colorful *"Boat House Row"* where Grace Kelly's brother rose to fame. Yeah, that Grace Kelly, the movie star and latter-day princess of Morocco, whose brick-layer father was eventually honored by the re-naming of East River Drive along the Schuylkill River into *"Kelly Drive."* The field where we played bordered Kelly Drive and was but four blocks away from the Philadelphia Zoological Gardens, the oldest zoo in the country.

(*"Ageless Body, Timeless Mind,"* by Deepak Chopra, M.D. *". . . con-jure up in your mind's eye one of the most wonderful moments of your childhood. . . a vivid scene of joy . . .[with] . . . you . . . the center of some activity . . .[I]intensely physical experiences are the easiest to use . . . By rejoining the flow of one magical instant, you trigger a transformation in your body. Signals . . . are activated . . . by memories and visual* *images. The more vivid your participation, the closer you will come to duplicating the body chemistry of that youthful moment. (*See pages 104-105*)*

(See Part IV next)

Shining Moment Sends Me Soaring High

YOU HAD TO BE A little tough to grow up in *Brewerytown,* the neighborhood of Philadelphia I called home the first part of my life. You also needed to be open to other ways of life, different religions, and those of another race.

Many of the kids I went to school with were *African-Americans.* Sometimes, I felt I fit in more with them then I did with some of the whites. I was an immigrant's son, different from the mostly northern European families; and I was a white minority, dark-skinned, ethnic curly-headed *Greek,* readily accepted by the mostly lower middle class group of black kids. I learned how to box in the school yard of *St. Ludwig's Roman Catholic Grade School. Blacks* taught me how to jab and punch, while keeping my guard up and being able to take a hit, while also learning how to hit back, just as hard.

We would not swing for the head, but simply *"slap"* lightly– *"upside the head"* — when an opening presented itself. I learned quickly, and soon took on kids outside our school who did not realize someone of my short stature would not back down, and would go toe-to-toe with them when they tried to bully me or my friends.

I also learned how to move, use *"dance steps"* as part of boxing. And just as important, how to *"weave"* and *"fake out"* an opponent. Keep in mind, North Philadelphia where I came from, has given the world some interesting athletic characters. *Johnny Weissmuller,* the greatest Tarzan of the Silver Screen and

Olympic Gold-medal swimming winner, came from old Columbia Avenue. *Joe Frasier*, the city's most famous boxer, still provides a gym with his name to train young men near Broad and Glenwood streets.

And *Bill Cosby*, one of America's best-loved funny men, came from one of the projects not far from my home. He was quite an athlete in his own right, playing collegiate football, and eventually earning a doctorate — a real one, not an honorary degree — in Physical Education from that North Philadelphia urban university at Broad Street and Montgomery Avenue, Temple University.

A 12-year-old's Shining Moment

A Fairmount player kicked off, and the football started to fall short. It came right toward me. I caught it, so proud that I could "*field it*" cleanly, but also have room to run in front of me. Somebody blocked the first tackler coming toward me, I veered to the left to avoid another, running along the right "*sidelines*" as a fellow from the other side — bigger than myself — got ready to make what's called an "*open field*" tackle.

I went right towards him, changing the ball from my right to my left arm, and getting as low as I could to the ground, ready to plow into him, in an attempt to knock him over. (I had "*a lot of heart*," they said, but also added I was a little *crazy*.) The tackler gets into his crouch, using quick speed to trick me into thinking he was going to hit me high near the ball carrying hand, when he actually "*duked me*" and went low.

He grabbed for my legs . . .

And never touched me.

I jumped in the air at the last possible moment, soaring upwards, hurdling his body as he fell face forward to the ground. I was in the air for only a millisecond or two. But it felt like a *Kodak Camera Moment* frozen in time. Both legs off the ground, arms swinging in front and back as I see only a blur to the side of me and toward the front.

I hear yelling, screaming. No, it's "cheering!" My teammates are urging me to go all the way.

I hit the ground and momentarily lose my balance, but recover, and dash a short distance untouched for the score. I will never forget that moment. Can't remember who won or lost. Or even what the score was at the end.

I do remember a friend, Jimmy Suss, re-telling this, my greatest sports adventure, to a young girl later that evening. Her name was Geraldine McFadden, whose heart I won the night before. I believe I had solidified my "*in with her*" through my "*athletic prowess.*" It was the second of three parts that made up the greatest weekend in my childhood years.

(See Part V next)

Remembering the greatest time of my Life

WHAT DOES A FIRST MEMORABLE kiss, scoring a break-away touchdown and opening to your Higher Self all have in common?

They occurred some time ago, but feel like it was only yesterday. The best weekend of my life, is how I see it now. But, you couldn't have told me when it was actually manifesting in the '60s.

I had met what I believed was the love of my life. I was all of 12 years old. Same age as Geraldine McFadden, the gymnast that *"flipped over me"* upon meeting at what today you would call a *"pre-teen"* party. Mostly 8th graders, but some older. I may have been the youngest.

After seeing this girl from 2nd and Allegheny streets (blocks and blocks away from my neighborhood in Brewerytown, North Philadelphia), I fell head over heels in love with her. (Well, she went head over heels. Did I mention she was a gymnast that *"flipped"* for me when I requested an example of her gymnastics?)

We eventually kissed in the darkened cellar where the party made its way. No adults allowed.

Soft *"oldies by goodies"* played in the background (the Jive Five, Dion and the Belmonts, and of course, *"16 Candles"* by the Crests).

The night ended too soon. I longed to be with Geraldine who stayed at her girlfriend's house for the weekend. But, I left for home, which was a half block from the party site — down Stiles Street and around the corner on 31st Street. (Some 40 blocks from where Gerry lived, but could have 40,000 blocks to a kid not used to taking a bus by himself, let alone drive a car.)

Energy created with Geraldine must have inspired something in me the next day, as I played football in Fairmount Park, scoring a touchdown after hurdling an opponent who stood (or actually, lowered himself to the ground to tackle me). He was the only obstacle to the goal line. I feel young every time I recall that exploit and the cheers I got. Oh, if only Ms. McFadden could have seen me! (Did we use the term *"Ms."* at that time? Don't think so.)

Uncertain if my true love would ever be mine, I fell to my knees the next day, praying for her affection. It was on a Sunday. I was scheduled to serve as an altar boy at St. Ludwig's Catholic Church. Got there early, and knelt upon a padded "kneeler" used mostly for "40-Hour" devotions, a Lenten thing, I believe. Wore a black cassock and a white surplus. Closed my eyes, bent my head and petitioned for Love.

I prayed for Geraldine McFadden's love. But got something far greater — the Love of God. Feeling so much pain, so much sorrow and an unbearable longing for the young girl, I know now that I had somehow entered another realm. Another consciousness.

The passage of time got lost. My yearning, desire and heart-ache came to an end. And I felt what I can only describe as the Presence of the Almighty. I was at peace. In love and receiving love right then and there. The one I had met at the party lost all relevance. I needed "nothing." Desired "nothing." I became "nothing." The "Nothing" mystics use to speak of their inability to describe their God, their Beloved, their Love.

It was a magical time, that weekend. The most memorable one of my life. The second most memorable time is when I remember that weekend with near total recall. Like . . . right . . . now.

Soft pretzels, a Philadelphia comfort food

"*YOU WANT MUTARD*," THE PRETZEL Man would ask as he took your nickel and broke off three little "*figure eight*" soft pretzels. "*Yes*," I'd say, mouthwatering for a topping that would make Philadelphia soft pretzels one of the great snacks of the Western World.

He was a small man, old beyond his years, wearing rumpled clothes that seemed two sizes too big for him. Always wore long sleeve shirts — dark colors — and a crumpled hat with sweat stains at the band.

His face was all gnarled up, like a flower with petals not ready to bloom. Kinda pinched together. Wrinkle upon wrinkle stretched across his dark and tanned weathered face.

Hands always appeared dirty. Particularly, the fingernails. Black gunk encrusted beneath the nails. They matched the black lines that branched out over old, calloused palms and across the inside of his wrists.

He couldn't pronounce the word, "*mustard*." Would leave off the "*s*" sound. Not sure if it was due to some injury or to a native language he spoke which could not easily adapt to and match our English sounds. Kids are cruel. We'd joke about the way he spoke; mimic him when he'd pass by, pushing his pretzel cart, with us parroting the words: "*you want mutard, you want mutard*."

The cart was a wooden one with two wooden wheels and "*push*" handles at the front. Wooden legs protruded from the bottom of the cart extending down from the handles above.

Glass encased the four sides of a "*box-like*" container. Looked like a big fish aquarium — only taller — with slats of wood attached to the four corners and the wooden top and bottom. This enabled us to "*see*" the pretzels. More importantly, it helped our Pretzel Man keep his products fresh and "*moist*," protected from the dry heat of summer. There' ain't nothing like a good soft pretzel with lots of wet chunks of course salt that blend into that unique pretzel dough flavor. The moist, the better! Fresher! Like they just rolled out the oven!

There's a number of foods Philadelphia has laid claim to: cheese steaks, scrapple, cream cheese, "Tastykakes," Herr's Potato Chips and hoagies. In my opinion, none compare to good old soft pretzels.

Never learned the nationality of our Pretzel Man. He walked the length of Brewerytown, returning to places like 30th and Stiles streets, meandering from Girard to Thompson streets, and northwards to the St. Ludwig's Catholic Church at 28th and Master Streets. All places where he could find customers like us, willing to overlook what would become today's standards of health and safety.

The Pretzel Man has gone the way of the ice-man, the guy that delivered big "*cinder block*" sizes of ice with tongs to houses with "*Ice boxes*." He was joined by the coal-delivery man, who poured little chunks of the black stuff into "*coal bins*" that stored the heat-producing resource in sections of cellars in our old row homes.

But, what I wouldn't give to see that Pretzel Man again, stopping his cart when he spies me and other neighborhood kids run up to him clutching nickels, dimes and quarters, in hopes of exchanging them for little pieces of good old-fashioned Philadelphia comfort food.

God bless those German monks that accidentally discovered how to make pretzels a few years earlier!

A tough road makes journey a little easier

~6~

WHEN MY FATHER SPOKE GREEK with the disciplinarian of the Catholic High School where I played hooky at age 14, I thought I had it made.

The Jesuit priest joked in the language I never learned, and the two laughed. They continued speaking Greek and I thought I'd get off with a warning, and not face a harsh punishment for cutting classes at Bishop Neumann High School in South Philadelphia. Our parish, St. Ludwig's Roman Catholic Church, was in North Philadelphia, but for some reason, students were required to travel some 45 minutes by bus. South Philly was "*foreign country* "to me and I felt treated as an outsider by the mostly Italian and Irish Catholics boys from there. You don't know how many fights I'd get into — always trying to prove my "*manhood*," and agreeing to meet a kid under some bridge where fair fights were conducted. It was a major reason I cut school. Not to run away from a fight, but to avoid getting into one.

The Greek priest and my Greek father finished talking, and I sat waiting the verdict. Got hit with the maximum sentence. *Twenty days detention.* Twenty days staying after school to think of the wrongs I committed, and to seek forgiveness from the Almighty. Twenty days in hostile territory where I had not one friend.

Students requiring discipline were ordered to appear at a special classroom at the school whose namesake, former Philadelphia Bishop John Neumann, would eventually be canonized, and the school's name changed to "*St. John Neumann*." Could never figure out the 19th century politics of the Catholic Church which permitted his remains to be buried in North Philadelphia, where I lived, and not South Philadelphia, where the fictional "*Rocky*" was depicted growing up. I visited his memorial (St. John Neumann, not Rocky) at a site near Fifth Street and Girard Avenue, near the old Schmidt's Brewery, and was disappointed when given one of the type of cards passed out at funeral homes with the deceased picture and his bio printed. I wanted a real live relic, the kind us Catholic were famous for providing the masses hundreds of years in our history.

Detention wasn't so bad. Got respect from some classmates who saw me in a new light. The tough kid who could take a punch and not complain. Got into no more fights the rest of the school year.

Also learned a fellow could "*work off*" his detention twice as fast if he was willing to endure some discomfort and apply himself. You'd get credit for two days of detention instead of one if you spent your hour kneeling rather than sitting on a chair in the classroom. I could do it, take the extra pain, and finish up my sentence quicker. I didn't know it at the time, but it set in motion a way of life that would do me well from then on. Enduring a little hardship now, for a greater reward later. Finishing the requirements for a bachelor's degree in three years rather than four years. Getting a master's degree in one year instead of two. Changing careers while approaching 40 and going to law school with kids nearly half my age, the toughest endeavor undertaken — and that includes attending Officer's Candidate School in Ft. Benning, Ga., and journeying in a place I learned the most about life, Vietnam.

Kneeling to a Higher Authority, even for an ulterior motive, showed me I could not only survive, but flourish in a world that often appeared to lack compassion. You have nowhere to go but up, once you rise from your knees and go forward.

II Philadelphia – City of Neighborhoods

PHILADELPHIA HAS BEEN CALLED THE City of Neighborhoods because of the many distinct sections that grew up over years as immigrants from all walks of life settled here and continued with their cultures from around the world. South Philly had many sections where Italians and Irish contributed their colorful lifestyles and religious beliefs, while North Philadelphia provided similar offerings from the Germans, the Welsh and the African Americans.

Names were given to each unique section. They included Academy Gardens, Andorra, Bella Vista, Brewerytown, Bridesburg, Burholme, Byberry, Callowhill, Cedar Park, Center City East, Chestnut Hill, Chinatown, Clearview, Crestmont Farms, Dickinson Narrows, Eastwick, East Falls, East Kensington, East Mount Airy, East Oak Lane, East Passyunk, East Poplar, Fairmount, Fishtown, Fitler Square, Fox Chase, Francisville, Franklin Mills, Garden Court, Germantown, Germantown – Westside, Germany Hill, Girard Estates, Graduate Hospital, Greenwich, Hawthorne, Holmesburg, Kensington, Lawndale, Lower Kensington, Lower Moyamensing, Logan Square, Mantua, Manayunk, Mayfair, Millbrook, Modena, Morrell Park, Newbold, Normandy Village, Northwood, Old City, Old Kensington, Olney, Overbrook, Oxford Circle, Packer Park, Parkwood Manor, Pennsport, Passyunk Square, Pennypack, Pennypack Park, Pennypack Woods, Point Breeze, Powelton, Queen Village, Rhawnhurst, Richmond, Rittenhouse, Riverfront, Roxborough Park, Spring Garden, Somerton, Spruce Hill, Society Hill, Stadium District, Summerdale,

Swamp Poodle, Tacony, Torresdale, Upper Roxborough, Walnut Hill, Washington Square West, West Central Germantown, West Passyunk, West Poplar, West Powelton, West Torresdale, Whitman, Winchester Park, Wissahickon, Wissahickon Hills, Wissinoming, Woodland Terrace, Wynnefield Heights and Yorktown.

The places that I hailed from – Fairmount and Brewerytown -- are still strong and thriving communities.

Fairmount

THE NAME "FAIRMOUNT" DERIVES FROM the hill where the Philadelphia Museum of Art is located and where William Penn intended to build his manor house. A handful of European settlers farmed the area from the 17th century through the early 19th century, when Fairmount was still outside Philadelphia's city limits. Prominent families established large estates there as well, including Bush Hill, White Hall, and Lemon Hill, the last of which still stands overlooking the Schuylkill River

During the American Revolution, British soldiers built defensive works on the hill of Fairmount. The purpose was to prevent American troops from attacking them from the north - the only side of the city not protected by water.

Three large institutions were located in the district in the 19th century. The first was the Water Works at the foot of Fairmount hill. The Water Works used waterpower to pump water from the Schuylkill River into reservoirs on the top of Fairmount hill, from where it flowed into city homes and businesses.

It was also an architectural and scenic attraction, according to national sources. Its buildings, which included a restaurant, were among the earliest examples of Greek revival architecture in the United States. Charles Dickens listed the facility as one of the two things he particularly wanted to see while in Philadelphia.

The other was Eastern State Penitentiary. The prison was the first in the country built specifically with the intention of reforming rather than simply punishing criminals. Intended to provide prisoners relief from the overcrowding and squalor of other prisons and give them time to reflect on their crimes, it led instead to intense despair and sometimes insanity among the inmates and was condemned by Dickens when he visited.

Fairmount is near the Philadelphia Museum of Art, with its famous "Rocky Steps" (immortalized in the 1976 Academy Award film, "Rocky.") It is located at the end of the Benjamin Franklin Parkway, a broad flag-lined street connecting City Hall to the Philadelphia Museum of Art. This stretch is known as the "Museum District." Along the Parkway are the Rodin Museum, Philadelphia's Central Library, the Franklin Institute of Science, the Academy of Natural Sciences and the Barnes Museum.

Brewerytown

WHILE BREWERYTOWN IS LISTED AS an "unofficial region," it runs between the Schuylkill River's eastern bank and 25th Street, bounded by Cecil B. Moore Avenue to the north and Parrish Street to the south. Brewerytown got its name because of the numerous breweries that were located along the Schuylkill during the late 19th century and early 20th century. It is now primarily a residential neighborhood, with a growing commercial sector along Girard Avenue.

Its legacy can be seen on maps from the 1860s, which list several minor brewers and distillation facilities in this region. Proximity to the river and of course nearby farmland allowed the establishments to flourish, and as demands increased, so did development in Brewerytown. Much of the expansion was handled by an architect named Otto Wolf, who oversaw the construction of over 60 buildings in the area, bringing a German texture to the houses, saloons, and breweries of the area. Some of his buildings are still standing, including the Bergdoll Brewing complex, and F.A. Poth Brewing.

(I asked a girl to go steady at age 14 while we smooching directly across from the old Bergdoll Brewery building. She said yes and I gave up all thoughts of becoming a priest at that time! In addition, the church I attended was St. Ludwig's Roman Catholic Church. It was named after a German saint and many of the families that had initially attended services there were of German descent.)

Columbia Park, the first home of the Philadelphia Athletics major league baseball team, was located at 30th and Oxford Streets in the neighborhood. The Athletics eventually made their way to Oakland and the city kept the National League team the Phillies.

> At its peak, 700 breweries operated across Philadelphia, several in a ten-block area of Brewerytown, according to a local Philadelphia history...

Unfortunately, with the collapse of local industry later in the 20th century, started by Prohibition in the United States, and beer production moving primarily to the Midwest, every single brewer had vanished by 1987. As of 2016, the only active brewery in Brewerytown is Crime & Punishment Brewing Company, which opened in 2015.

During this slump, the entirety of North Philadelphia, Brewerytown included, was hit hard by economic depression, white flight and other factors. Much of the area was deemed blighted by the city government. For the last few decades, Brewerytown has been a predominantly poor, African-American neighborhood.

In 1991, the Brewerytown Historic District was certified by the National Register of Historic Places. The district contains 380 buildings and is roughly bounded by 30th St., Girard Ave., 32nd St. and Glenwood Ave.[

Breweries that operated in the neighborhood included:

- Bergner & Engel Brewing Company (Thompson Street between 32nd and 33rd, east side)
- Charles Eisner Brewery (Thompson Street between 32nd and 33rd, west side)
- F. A. Poth Brewing Company (31st & Jefferson Streets, NW corner)
- H. Mueller Centennial Brewery (31st & Jefferson Streets, NE corner)
- J. & P. Baltz Brewing Company (31st & Thompson Streets)

- Arnholt & Schaefer Brewing Company (31st and Thompson Streets, NE corner)
- G. Keller's Brewery (31st Street, west side, between Jefferson and Master)
- J. Bentz' Brewery (31st Street, west side, between Jefferson and Master)
- Thomas Perot Brewery (31st and Master Streets, NW corner)
- W. S. Perot (32nd and Thompson Streets, NW corner)
- Goldbeck & Eisele (31st and Thompson Streets, NE corner)
- Geo. F. Rothacker Brewery (31st Street, West side, between Thompson and Master)
- Eble & Herter (33rd Street and Pennsylvania Avenue)
- Francis Orth (later Burg & Pfaender, later Bergdoll Brewery; 33rd Street, south of Master Street)
- Henzler & Flach Brewery
- City Park Brewery (29th and Parrish Streets)
- Commonwealth Brewing Company (28th and Cambridge Streets)
- Keystone State Brewery (27th and Parrish Streets)
- Peter Schemm and Son (West College Ave. and Poplar Street)
- India Pale Ale Brewery (38th Street and Girard Avenue)
- Michel Gosse (27th & Thompson Streets)

Brewerytown never too far behind me

No matter where I go, Philadelphia will always go with me. I've taken the old neighborhood to combat in Vietnam as well as to the Wailing Wall in Jerusalem. I let it shine in the courthouses of Philadelphia and the one and only house of pleasure I visited in Panama.

Yeah, I'm from Brewerytown, an old German-based section of Philadelphia that families of beer-makers settled in a small enclave of the City of Brotherly Love. Brewerytown is near the Philadelphia Zoo on Girard Avenue and not too far from the Eastern State Penitentiary where Al Capone once lived in a section called Fairmount.

> Brewerytown was a thriving community once upon a time, but it went downhill as Prohibition set in and the neighborhood lost its livelihood but not its unique nature. There are no more breweries there despite the appeal of the 21st Amendment that was based on something historians called the Volstead Act. (I think a bunch of do-gooders got together to do away with "rum and Romanism" and the "righteous" way of life places like my hometown provided its people and their culture. We had more breweries and delivery beer facilities in our small patch of land than any other in Pennsylvania and maybe the entire East Coast.)

I learned to sing and dance in old Brewerytown. My African-American brothers taught me that in the school yard of a Catholic Church grounds called St.

Ludwig's. (What would you expect from a German parish at the turn of the 20th century? We fondly called it "Dutch Louie's!")

My Irish Catholic girlfriend showed me everything I would ever want to know about love while across the street from one of the old breweries. (She agreed to go steady with me at age 14, and I've gone steady with no one since giving her my high school ring back then.)

You see, I am the same fellow today that I was back then and it just goes to prove the old saying:

"You can take the kid out of the old neighborhood, but you'll never take the old neighborhood out of the kid."

Escaping Brewerytown in 1 piece not easy

I NEVER TOOK MY EYES off the gun. The man's hand shook. I was afraid it would go off. Raising my own hands, I prayed that he would not shoot, and said "*I'm coming out*," slowly climbing out of the window, placing one foot on the ground and then the other as I exited the ACME supermarket warehouse building two blocks from my home.

Two other teens followed, each hoping the old gray-haired man in the rumpled uniform would not lose his cool and hurt someone. The security guard caught us leaving the building. It was the second time in an hour that six of us — ages 13 to 15 — had meandered through the six-story building and made our way to the roof where we filled shopping bags with "*halfies*," parts of round "pimple balls" that had split and enabled us to play "*half ball*." In the 50s, 60s and 70s, urban kids played a version of baseball using one-half of a round inflated rubber ball that had been damaged and eventually cut in half. The entire ball was called a "*whole ball*," which we'd play with until it sprung a leak. We'd trim the "*heads*" off of brooms and mops, and simply use the handles as bats and played against a backdrop of buildings, sometime row homes, or in this case, the six-story ACME building.

> Hit a half-ball over the roof and it was a home run. Both sides would agree that a ball hit over a certain mark, say the top of a window near the roof, was a triple, and the top of the lower window a double. Anything below was a single.

That is, if it bounced off the wall after being struck and no one caught it. A player was out if the other side caught the ball off the wall. You'd be called out if you'd hit the halfie and it never made it from the pavement where you stood, to the other side of the street and struck the building's wall (or window!) And of course, three strikes and you'd be out.

No one, I mean no one, had ever gotten to the roof of the ACME building until that day when someone left open a rear window at the 31st and Master streets facility in Brewerytown, Philadelphia.

That includes all of the *"old head."* Those fellows — who at that time were in their late teens and early to mid-20s — who came before us and played at the same site. Former *"30th Streeters,"* members of a gang who shot zip guns at each other for fun in nearby Fairmount Park. Or the *"Green Street Counts"* who roamed the Fairmount section long before Rocky Balboa ran up the steps of the area's most famous landmark. Let's not forget the African American gangs, *"2-8,"* which stood for the 28th Street blacks that dominated to the north, or the notorious members of the *"Valley,"* who won't tell anyone today, more than 50 years after the fact, where some bodies were placed. No statute of limitations on a homicide.

But, we were good and clean kids who lived near 31st Street and Girard Avenue, a major thoroughfare of North Philadelphia. None of us were members of any gang. We were into sports and athletics. It just so happened we were in the wrong place at the wrong time when the guard got a radio call and drew his gun and arrested the three of us, while the others got away.

I'll never forget what happened. And, the lesson I learned when our parents were subpoenaed and appeared in juvenile court for our *"criminal"* behavior. But, that's a story for another the next post coming up!

(See Part II next)

'Do the right thing' – do what's right for you

THE MOMENT OF TRUTH CAME down to one question: "*Who else was with you?*"

I looked to the floor and didn't answer until the head of a juvenile aid panel from Philadelphia Family Court asked me to speak up.

I dare not raise my eyes. I had to "*come clean*" and admit my fault. But, I was uncertain whether I should involve someone else. So many thoughts went through me. Be the good altar boy who wanted to be a priest, and tell of all six who entered the property, going from floor to floor to get to the roof and back.

We were looking at the charge of burglary, entering property of another without permission to commit a crime therein. "*Breaking and entering*" is another term used, but we actually broke nothing and simply climbed through a window of a 4-story building three blocks from my Brewerytown, North Philadelphia, home to retrieve half balls hit onto the roof.

Tell them, I thought. You know who was there. They caught you and two of your friends. But they wanted the others. Those kids were older, at least two years senior of my age of 13. I'm the youngest. I shouldn't be the dumbest.

Do the right thing!

Other voices spoke to me, however. Came from James Cagney, Edward G. Robinson, Humphrey Bogart and the "*tough*" guys in the movies I admired. They played the hoods, the gangsters, the "*bad guys*" who I looked up to, who knew what to do. (Never "*rat out*" a friend.)

Give up the names of others in this "*criminal conspiracy?*" Trespassing in order to remove hundreds of halfies that blanketed the roof top structure. That's what we did, and I admit it.

Hell, half of the halfies were no good. They were split or had melted from years in the hot sun. Others were caked with tar that must have "*bled*" during the really hot days.

"*Who else was with you, Michael Contos?*" asked the woman again. She was the head of the panel and sat in the middle, flanked by two others at a long table facing me and the other boys who sat directly across the room from them. Our parents (my mother) appeared in Court and sat behind us.

"*I don't know,*" I said. It was a heartfelt answer. And I felt it was right. Until Dave *(not his real name)* named my best friend, Johnny Keller, as one of those not caught. *J* then named another, Billy McLaughlin, the good Irish kid who lived around the corner near 30th and Stiles streets.

Not sure if it was the right thing to do, but I felt safe. The panel had no reason to think I knew either one of those named. But, there was a report of three kids, not two, that escaped from a gun-toting elderly security guard who rounded up us miscreants. The juvenile aid chair would settle for nothing less than all co-conspirators.

She asked again. "*Who else was with you?*" Confident with my deception, I spoke louder, putting an innocent plea in my voice, "*I don't know, I told you.*"

Dave gave the same answer, but with less conviction, refusing to, or being unable to, make eye contact with the panel. And then they got to Joey (*also not a real name*).

"*Johnny Contos*," he said, naming my older brother.

Silence followed. It was a deadly silence, I seemed to recall.

I felt her, more than I actually saw her, as the juvenile official directed her gaze toward me. She caught me. Caught me in a lie.

"*You don't know you're own brother?*" the woman said with a touch of pity . . . and . . . what I would later describe as pure disdain.

The state declined to bring charges against us. It was the right thing to do. Don't know if I did the "*right thing*" back then. Hate to say it, but even after all the years and the so-called wisdom I was supposed to gain with age, I'd probably do the same thing again.

May not have been *the* "*right*" thing to do. But, it was right thing for **me**.

Hit upside the head provides a life lesson

The detective hit me across the face with a back hand and I knew I was in trouble. Blood formed on my lower lip. I let it flow, not taking my eyes from this man who gained my immediate attention with a force he evidently knew how to use on some wise-ass kid not being straight with him.

WE WERE IN THE BATHROOM of a union hall where my best friend's brother was celebrating his marriage earlier in the day. I was 13 or 14 and had just "hit" several cars in the parking lot, opening unlocked doors for spare change and cigarettes when I came across this large caliber handgun. It was sitting on the console of the car in plain sight.

I tucked it into my suit pants and I entered the hall, going straight to the bathroom. That's when I started to show off my "*find*" to someone I knew and failed to look around the rest of the room, where one of Philadelphia's finest — a detective in civilian clothes and one of the wedding guests – saw the gun and decided to investigate.

"*Where did you get that?*" this tall, muscular blonde policeman said to me, his steely eyes watching not only what I said but how I said it. "*I found it,*" I quipped, as I try to turn away from him.

Wham! He hit me and demanded I tell him the truth. Which I did. In a roundabout way without spilling the beans about my latest spree as a juvenile delinquent. Somehow I knew even then there were certain things not to divulge to a police officer without a lawyer present.

"It was lying in plain sight and I just took it from a car," I said in all sincerity, not mentioning the other petty thefts I attempted. Stealing a gun is a felony offense in Philadelphia, I later learned as a criminal defense lawyer. Using one in a crime calls for a mandatory sentence of five to 10 years in jail. Unless you're a juvenile. Then the state gets to control your living arrangements up to age 21, in some cases.

I relinquished the gun, wishing I had never come to the wedding reception, let alone try to get away with possessing a firearm. I got scared. My future looked bleak. I fell back on the only thing I could think of to help.

I started praying. Praying so hard the vibrations might rival a Gabriel blowing his horn in the Old Testament. And, it worked. The officer spoke to Eddie Keller, the fellow who just got married who *"vouched"* for me, saying I was a good kid. *"A little stupid, at times,"* he said, smiling at me with the cop on one side and my best friend, Johnny Keller, on the other.

Don't know what happened to the gun. Nobody pressed charges. I feel some Divine intervention had taken place keeping me out of more trouble or a loss of life at a possibly young age.

Corporal punishment has had its place in our society. Never forgot the lesson I learned. Guns are nothing to play with. Particularly in the hands of such a dumb kid as yours truly.

Radio Plays to My No. 1 Heart's Desire

MUSIC TOUCHED AN EMOTIONAL CHORD in me that may have been different from most folks.

I was only twelve when I got exposed to it. I felt such a swelling up of sadness and joy as certain songs played on the radio. I'd sit for hours. Alone. Just me and an old-fashioned radio positioned on the kitchen table. I'd close my eyes and sing along, knowing the words to the most soulful and heart-wrenching music of the day. And when my folks got concerned, questioning my solitary activity, I'd leave the room, seeking another outlet, another radio in a secluded spot elsewhere.

There was one station that would play the top-20 hits of the week. It was an African American radio station, WDAS in Philadelphia. Not sure if the disc jockey was Georgie Woods, the *"man with the goods,"* or *Jocko Henderson*. The record *"Puppy Love,"* a song by a local group, had just came out, and I'd call in everyday asking those at the station to play it. It got so popular for the North Philadelphia listeners that it climbed all the way to number one with my voice being used over the radio that week with one of the many call-in requests.

I didn't know someone was taping all phone calls into the radio station at the time. I had never heard my voice played back before, although I should have guessed something was going on when I heard other fans speak via the box. This is in the days before stereo, the days of *"Hi Fi,"* whatever that meant. Reception was usually *"not bad"* on a good day, and *"really bad,"* on other days, depending on the time of the day.

The top 20 countdown had gone all the way to nineteen, and I felt rejected. I took it personal that my song, *Puppy Love*, by Little Jimmy and the Tops, never made it. I put my head down, cradling it on the arms that covered the table. I felt so low, the floor beneath looked mighty inviting for me to spend the rest of my Life.

And then I heard it. *"This is Michael Contos,"* a scratchy-sounding recording played over the radio. I froze. In shock. Nearly jumping from the chair, I wanted so badly to run outside and shout it to the world that I was on the Radio! *"That's me you're hearing,"* I wanted to grab people on the street and scream it into their faces. "It's my request they're playing."

Puppy Love was Number 1!

It was the most popular song of the week!

The request lasted just a few seconds. But the smile I get remembering that moment has lasted for years.

To top it off, I became a small celebrity when appearing in the eighth grade class at St. Ludwig's grade school in Brewerytown the next day. One of the most beautiful girls in the class, Diane Kleinschmidt, smiled at me and told me, rather confidentially, that she had heard me on the radio the night before. I was speechless. This gorgeous 12-year-old never looked in my direction before this day. Here, she was making eye contact with me in a way I had not felt before. On the inside. Or the outside.

She likes me, I thought. She really likes me.

Too late. She had started to date JoJo Guiliano, a guy that Philadelphia's Rocky might have been modelled had Sylvester Stallone ever met him. Diane and he married and lived happily ever after for a while.

So did my memory of *Puppy Love* and my brief moment in the spotlight.

Pitching pennies provides pinch per police

CORNER LOUNGING. POLICE PICKED US up more times than I can remember simply for *hanging out* and making a little too much noise, perhaps, with a little too much profanity.

I didn't. Use profanity. Not much. And when I did, I think it meant something. Not like today, when the "*F*" word is bantered around too freely. And way too often. And, that's in so-called "*polite society*."

We were young kids drawn to older kids who had little to occupy their time except hang out in our geographic circles, aka, the street corner. The "*coolest*" ones, the teenagers with the nice outfits and a quip for anything anti-establishment, got the most attention and adulation. I looked up to those "*old heads*" who could cuss up a storm and strut their stuff in walking down a street. *And those were just the girls!*

Like *Midge Connerton*. I think she was the first of the opposite sex that I noticed was more of a woman than a girl. Seem to always wear oversized sweat shirts (probably belonged to "*Beanie*" her brother) and jeans that rolled up at the end. Smoked cigarettes. And caused kids like me, two to three years younger than her, to look up to her as both a "*roll*" model, and a model you wouldn't mind "*rolling*" around with.

She was cute. And had breasts. At age 14, they stood out. They got attention, is what I mean. You put them in the mix with corner-lounging, cursing and smoking, and you got yourself a one-way ticket to juvenile delinquency and teenage pregnancy, is what our parents thought. We viewed it as juvenile delicacies and teenage prep for adulthood.

Good kids for the most part, cops would label all as trouble-makers, running us in, based on some flimsy complaint with the hope of scaring us off the corners. We'd go right back after our parents would "*bail us out*" of the police precincts, lecturing us, as we'd swear before the Almighty we'd never do again whatever it was we were accused of doing in the first place.

My mother learned about this "*police work*" the hard way. Four or five of us barely into our teens were "*pitching*" pennies outside of our house at 31st Street and Girard Avenue in Brewerytown, Philadelphia. My brother, *John*, and I were using pennies we got from a jar my mother was saving them in. Charlie Dell A'Casa, our next door neighbor, used his own pennies as did the other kids, all ranging from twelve to 14. (I was the youngest.)

A "*red car*" drove up the wrong way of 31st Street and pulled onto the pavement as two police officers jumped out of police car — all in red at that time — and rounded us up, grabbing the pennies lying on the pavement as evidence of our crimes. None would listen to what any of us had to say. Got threatened by one of the cops to shut up "*or else*," as he indicated with body language what he would do with the club he carried on him.

Mom heard the racket inside the house, came out, and the last I seen her, she was holding open the screen door, shouting at the cops "*They were my pennies. I gave them to 'em to play!*"

Did no good. The law is the law. And a complaint is a complaint, no matter what or where it may have originated. Or whether it was ever founded or not.

We got released. But got no lecture from our folks this time. Never did "*pitch*" pennies again. The object was to get as close to the wall with your penny to win. We played the game with a deck of cards instead of money from then on. Learned to move our "*corner-lounging*" away from those corners that gathered the most complaints too. It was all part of the learning process in growing up in the city. Tough but educational. Just like Life.

A 'Lot of Heart' can go a long way in life!

Kids I grew up with in the tough section of North Philadelphia said that I had "a lot of heart." I cherish that statement more than any I later heard as a teenager, a young adult or even someone in his middle ages looking back on what made him the most proud in his short lifetime. You'd have a "lot of heart" if you didn't care for the consequences when sticking up for a black kid when a white "friend" called him the "N" word and then classified you as a "N-gger lover" for coming to his defense.

It didn't happen often. I'd feel hurt that someone would say that to me, but felt even worse for the kid the ignorant white son-of-a-bitch tried to belittle. I learned that the ignorance was passed down from father to son in a way to make them feel better than another group of persons — like Nativist Americans felt about Catholics in our country's history. I didn't like them and preferred the company of guys who cared more for who you were than the color of your skin or the country your immigrant father came born.

Blacks taught me how to box, how to swear and how to enjoy life by not taking it too seriously. They said I had "a lot of balls" and that I was "cock-strong" because I could take a punch and dish out as much as I could take. I loved the music they'd listen to on the radio station, WDAS in Philadelphia, as Georgie Woods, *"the guy with the goods"* would play what was labelled as "race" music and later called "Doo Wop" music. I envied how they sang and danced, and eventually learned to harmonize with a white group that later appeared on television, and really mixed it up at dances doing such old-time favorites as the "Slop," the "Mashed Potatoes" and the "Stomp."

But having heart usually meant you'd fight for the right cause. That you would "do the right thing" as Spike Lee would later say. Even if it meant "duking it out" with someone three years older than you at the tender age of twelve. I refused to back down when Billy Van Horn tried to boss me and a bunch of black kids playing on Harper Street in a section of Philly called Brewerytown. Blacks primarily lived north of that area divided by Girard Avenue, and whites on the south toward Ogden Street where the Van Horns lived in the predominantly white section called Fairmount.

I don't remember the details, but I didn't run or cower when Billy came at me. He had confidence that most kids would let him have his way. But I didn't. And that's when we fought.

We fought from one side of the small street to the other. Harper Street is a single lane road with parking on one side. There was a World War II Memorial at the far end of the street, just beyond the iron fences that prevented anyone from crossing onto the property of the railroad that passed beneath the Girard Avenue Bridge not far from the Philadelphia Zoo three blocks away.

I remember nearly tripping when he backed me up from the pavement on the south side to the one on the north. I don't know where I found the strength, but I swung harder than I ever swung when I felt I was literally up against the brick wall of one of the single-family row homes. Soon I forced him back across the street and onto the other pavement where he stopped fighting and called it quits. He made light of the fight and said he was only playing. But I surely was not and I don't think any of the kids witnessing the fight — both white and black — agreed with him.

I didn't realize that I had earned somewhat of a reputation after that episode. A few days later I had gone to the top of Lemon Hill in Fairmount Park when a white fellow who was a friend of the Van Horns tried to push me away. One of Billy's brother told the kid — Tommy Humphrey — that I had fought Billy, and Humphrey not only backed off, but befriended me with a hearty smile and some corny jokes.

Looking back, I see that I dove into new challenges in my later years, becoming an infantry platoon leader in Vietnam, writing as a newspaper reporter and trying to help the downtrodden as both a union organizer and later a Philadelphia public defender. I couldn't have done it if I didn't believe they were the right causes in which to fight for at the time. Having a lot of heart has helped me become someone I think my old neighborhood friends would be proud of today.

Joseph Lachawiec:

Mike, I know you feel the fight was long and hard, however, what you may not recall is your bunch came down 30th Street to use the ball field in the park instead of crossing Over Girard Avenue Bridge, then Poplar Drive. Since your guys had baseball equipment, the bats struck fear in our hearts as your guys were brazen enough to come through our territory.

Yes the fight was tough but necessary in order to sort out the pecking order. No one was supposed to get seriously hurt. Billy was a tough kid but he was very skinny and weighed about 90 pounds.

If Big Ed fought you, the signal to your guys would have made us seen as enemies forever; but we all liked your bunch and got along well.

I dated a B'town girl one summer. I walked her home as she lived around 29th & Thompson streets. I got jumped by five black kids all of whom had half ball bats. I was able to hold my own for a while as I took a bat from one of the kids but I got whacked over the left eye by another. This set me off and I started chasing them up 29th Street, but as I did so, an older black man grabbed me and warned me not to go further as more were waiting to ambush me.

I turned for home and an ice pack.

I still have a knot on my head from that altercation.

All in all, our neighborhoods were great places to grow up and learn about the way of the world.

Contoveros:

I'm sorry to hear about the altercation you had with some kids who chased and hit you Joe. It's never right for someone to attack another with no provocation and I'm glad that you were able to hold your own and get in a whack at one of the little bastards.

> I felt comforted when hearing that the elderly black fellow had come to your aid and warned you against further trouble. I believe he represented the great majority of folks, both white and black, who don't want to see people hurt because they're different than others.

Corresponding with you here has been enlightening! I never knew anyone who had witnessed my fight with Billy Van Horn and it just goes to show that the Universe conspires in many ways to keep us guessing about our true purpose in life.

Growing up in the old neighborhoods of Philadelphia was indeed a great lesson, one I hope others can realize when they reflect on their early *"misadventures."*

Dance floor good place to learn to play ball

Two girls fought over me once.

Well, it really wasn't me that caused the fight. It was my dance steps.

You see, in the 1960s, I was only one of few guys that learned how to dance the *"Mashed Potatoes,"* the dance started by *"fellow"* Philadelphian Dee Dee Sharp. It was just like the *"Slop,"* another dance I had picked up which called for similar footwork.

I attended a dance every Sunday night at "Saint Joe's" at 16th and Allegheny streets, a section of North Philadelphia where Catholic priests ran an orphanage for boys. Never met any of the orphans, but it did give us kids from Brewerytown a chance to stay out of trouble and mingle with the opposite sex.

Most guys simply *"hung out,"* trying to be *"cool."* Lucky if they even danced a slow dance. Wanted to just look and be seen, I guess.

Not me. My father would lead the *"Greek Snake Dance"* at weddings and parties, and he must have been a good role model, because I never felt shy about trying to dance. Or appearing like a fool if I failed.

Guys would create a special routine as *"Mashed Potato Time"* played. Two or three of us would pretend we were ballplayers. One, like my good friend from

St. Ludwig's School – Bobby Richmond who later became a Philadelphia police officer -- was a batter, while another was a pitcher or a catcher.

> I'd go into a *"wind-up"* with my arms waving over my head, the whole time *"mashing"* my feet together in tune with the song. I pretended to throw a ball and the other dancer would swing and either miss or hit the pretend ball.

> If you were really good, you'd do a *"split:"* fall to the dance floor with both legs *"splitting"* out like two halves of a scissors. You wouldn't be all stretched out from the groin on down, but merely give the "appearance" they were extended that way.

> I could do a split!

And that's what got the attention of two girls who vied with each other to dance with me. One was a girl named Marty, a year older than me. Didn't know her. Only learned of her name later. She was a cute brunette who danced with style, occasionally making eye contact with an inviting smile. Never followed up. Too shy in that department.

But some other girl either pushed or bumped Marty out of the way to dance across from me. She didn't last long. Marty shoved back, nearly knocking the girl to the floor. More shoving followed and before you knew it, somebody grabbed somebody's hair. And the fight was on!

I stopped dancing as others around me also came to a halt, watching the girls go at it. Friends of the girls broke it up and the last I heard the two were agreeing to meet afterwards *"to settle things."*

They never did, as far as I know. And I was willing to dance with both if they only picked up the baseball dance routine. Don't need to fight when you to learn to play ball with each other. Found that out on the dance floor.

November 22, a day like no other day!

_____&

I REMEMBER THE TRAGIC NEWS just as if it was yesterday. My 10th grade American mathematics teacher whispers the horrible news: "*Somebody shot the president.*"

Panic starts, spreading quickly through the class room. Everyone is talking, particularly those who only hear part of the news.

Someone asks her, my favorite teacher, to repeat what was overheard. "*The President has just been shot,*" She says. Her face now becoming ashen white.

Oh my God, one student, an African-American girl, says as she holds her hands to her face. I never saw so much anguish as I did on that girl's pretty young face. She starts to cry. Others talk. They talk over each other. The noise gets louder. You can't hear yourself think, everyone is talking what sounds like "*gibberish*" and for the first time in my young life I think I understand what the word, "chaos," actually means. There seems to be no escape from complete and utter disorder.

Next, our confident and normally strong teacher — Miss Kelly — is restoring a little calm, raising her voice to get our attention, telling us to gather our school things, to leave the classroom and to go to the auditorium.

All classes at Dobbins Technical Institute, a trade school here in Philadelphia, PA, are merging together in assembly. No one knows why. Must be a speaker or an important video for us to see, I think. It couldn't have anything to do with something so far removed from us as, what might be happening outside of school, my home town, my own little world. Could it?

The wooden seats are uncomfortable to sit in, as everyone is squirming around, talking in our low voices. No one seems to know why we are gathering together, this November 22nd, in the Year of Our Lord, Nineteen Hundred and Sixty-Three.

And then it happens. I am sitting closer to my history teacher than any other student. We are separated from the rest of my class. Alone. Another teacher, a former football player who now teaches trigonometry, has just said something to her that I can't quite make out. My teacher turns to me. I can still see her long, dark hair and the dark glasses that she would peer over when trying to challenge us with a question or two. I admit now that I had a crush on her, but I never told anyone. That's one reason I went to graduate school and obtained a masters' degree in American History. She helped me believe in history, and more importantly, she helped me to believe in myself.

What she says as she turns her eyes to me, her glasses now removed from her face, as she focuses all of her adult vision toward me, a kid, ten days shy of his 14th birthday, I will remember 'til the day I die.

"*The president is dead,*" she says, as her voice cracks slightly, a far cry from the usual professional tone she offers in our classes.

John F. Kennedy, the youngest person ever to be elected president of the United States of America, is killed on this day in November of 1963.

It means more to me now than Thanksgiving Day will ever mean during the month of November. More than Veterans Day. More than All Saints' Day. More than . . . ah, to hell with Black Friday!

I remember this day as another American generation will recall "9 – 11;" recall what they ("we") were doing and where we were when the airplanes crashed into the twin towers.

Why does tragedy always stand out so much?

Perhaps, to remind us a moment "*in time*" can last a "*life time.*"

And that we can recall it decades later, perhaps with a little more love, compassion and understanding.

Injustice should make us all 'go berserk'

"GOING BERSERK" HAS ALWAYS HAD a wicked appeal to me.

For brief moments, I'd go *"mad,"* and not care for my safety or well-being, but focus instead on the object causing a *"crazy re-action"* on my part. It was as if a volcano had erupted and I wanted to punish those perceived as evil-doers. Might have had a bit of *"religious fervor"* involved, as I saw myself correcting a wrong or an injustice with a quick upper-cut to the jaw.

One of the first times I felt this way, was while in high school, maybe 16 years old. A bully was threatening Tommy Cannon, a guy from my neighborhood studying plumbing at Dobbins Technical High School, Philadelphia, where I learned printing. Had just gotten to know Tom. He was a tall, lanky guy, with a dry sense of humor and a quick wit. Was smart, too. Shared a belief in what was important in life, and learned that friendship ranked right up there with God and family.

Saw some *"tough"* kids surround Tommy and I went *"berserk"* when one demanded money from him. I crossed a distance of 20 feet in no time, jumping into the air as I got closer to the bully, thinking of nothing except helping my new friend.

I remember how time slowed down. I had pulled both legs from beneath me and slowly aimed them at this menacing youth leading the harassment. Saw myself as one of those Kung Fu fighters in the movies where someone pauses the action so audiences could see the impact of the oncoming blow to an opponent's head.

Never tried this before, and did not have a chance to analyze what I was doing while in the air. A frenzy of sorts had taken over me. I felt I could not let anything bad happen to my friend even if it meant a greater harm to myself. I didn't care!

Halfway toward the assailant, I saw him glance at me from the corner of an eye. I saw fear. I saw the emotion he sought to elicit from his latest victim. I saw a punk, a coward who felt "*big*" only by making others feel "*small.*"

At the last possible moment — while still suspended in the air traveling with the break-neck speed from such a long running-jump — I . . . felt . . . pity. Pity for a guy who needed to act in such a way for attention . . . for camaraderie . . . for some love he probably did not receive at home.

I pulled my legs closer to my body, tucked them beneath me, and aimed both knee caps in the general direction of this kid who was bigger than Tommy and myself. Instead of aiming for his head, I directed the blow to his body, knowing this would still knock him on his ass. Both knees struck his upper side. The momentum pushed him far away from Tommy, and caused a "*shock wave,*" to hit the other bad kids who had surrounded Tom. They quickly, and silently, moved away from such unexpected violence.

I had fallen to the concrete school floor, and immediately stood up, shouting "*What the hell happened!*" pretending ignorance and mistake. "*I'm sorry man,*" I said to the fallen bully. "*I thought someone was trying to hurt my boy here.*" I extended my hand and helped him to his feet. He seemed dazed. Speechless. I had hurt a lot more than his feelings, but he said nothing, probably confused with what just happened.

And then it was over. No retaliation. No "*dirty*" looks from any of the tough kids. Tommy had been as surprised as I was when I went a little crazy, and we never talked about it in school of when back in the neighborhood of Brewerytown. *"Going berserk"* is something I have had to control all my life, letting it loose while in a battle on the fields of Vietnam or in the courtrooms of Philadelphia. And since I am not writing from a prison or a forced labor camp today, I guess I've finally gotten a good handle on it.

Dobbins Reunion manifests HS aging story

As SOON AS ANY OF us turned 18 and got a draft card, we'd rushed to the printing shop at Dobbins Technical Institute, also known as Dobbins High School, and commenced to committing a federal offense punishable by up to 10 years in prison.

I didn't know it was against the law, but I guess I should have known you can't change the date of birth on your Selective Service card to show you're 21 years old rather than 18. But, it was the best way of getting served in every Philadelphia bar.

Yeah, I graduated from high school 50 years ago. I also learned that one could skirt the rules and have fun learning how you to deal with something called adulthood.

Getting credentials for the legal drinking age was one way!

> We'd get the small draft card and place it in the center of a large camera. No, not the Polaroid kind, but one called a Process Camera that used high intensity lamps to shine on the image you wanted to reproduce. You'd then dial equations to enlarge the printed area l.

> Once you done that, you "print" a copy onto a negative. Get the negative and then "opaque out" the section of the card that shows the date of birth.

For instance, if your birth date is 12-01-1948, you'd block it out and make a copy of a smaller version of the card. That smaller version would show an empty slot.

The next step was as easy as typing with a keyboard. You just put in a new date that shows you are at least 21, such as 12-01-1945.

Dobbins also offered me a career in regular printing, which I worked at before being drafted and serving in the army. I became a journalist and used a lot of what I learned in high school for designing newsletters and small newspapers.

It came in handy when starting a Blog and wanting to jazz it up a little to make it easier to read with artwork, some italicized words, and the choice of font size and style.

The statute of limitations has long passed and my own legal reasoning tells me that my confession here will not force me back in jail. (I hope not!) It will just remind a lot of my high school friends how crazy we once were and can now look back and laugh at our fun-loving childish ways.

Big Moose bar helps wayward boys to grow

MY MOTHER HIT ME UPSIDE the head when she caught me drinking beer in the Big Moose bar up the street from where we lived.

I was 16 years old at the time and sipping a Ballantine beer with a friend from Dobbins Technical High School. Someone must have ratted me out as my good friend Joe Walsh and I — both young white guys — drank in the African American bar in a section of Philadelphia called Brewerytown.

Joe was a year ahead of me in school and had just introduced me to what he called a "Sneaky Tine." That's a Ballantine beer with a shot of red liquor mixed in.

I never got a chance to drink more than a taste of the beer when my mom entered the bar, dragged me out and started to hit me on the head. "Is that's what you do with the money I give you?" she shouted at me in the early evening hours. It was still light out and all I kept thinking was of the humiliation I felt in full view of everyone I believed watched it.

I could have told mom I was spending my own money which I made as a messenger boy at a printing place in center city. But I kept my mouth shut and took the punishment like a man. Embarrassed, but a little wiser.

Big Moose played an important role in my oldest brother's passage to adulthood. George and a bunch of older teenagers had broken into the bar and stole beer and soda. He was the only one caught and was given a chance by a judge whether to go to jail or got into the army. He chose the latter and made a 22-year-year career out of the military. He helped to pave the way for me to become an officer in the army years later with both of us ending up in Vietnam at different times in our lives. (Meanwhile, my drinking buddy, Joe Walsh, became a homicide detective in the City of Brotherly Love.)

The bar no longer exists. The building has been converted into what looks like a small apartment complex. Driving past it the other day I couldn't help but recall how much it played in lives of my brother and me. It provided us with a "rite of passage" of sorts. It helped to make us grow into the salvageable men I believe we later became.

Harmony of 'The Wind' Still Warms Me

"Wind... Wind... Blow Wind...
...Oooooh Oooh...
...Blow Wind...!"

YOU COULDN'T HELP BUT MELT while listening to the old singing group offer its beatific sounds to the young teenagers dancing at Saint Joe's Sunday night dance special.

The girls loved the soft harmonies that whispered about their longing for true love. While boys, like me, sang the back-up parts, attempting to harmonize with our African American brothers who introduced us to a form of Rock & Roll which would later be called "Doo Wop."

Saint Joseph's Orphanage for boys is still operating there in North Philadelphia, but there are no more dances. Doo Wop is a song of the past. But I'll always remember it whenever I hear the sounds of yesterday and the love it brings to my heart and to my mind . . .

The song called "The Wind" was a special one that lifted me to a higher level of consciousness. I felt I existed on a different plane, one where love, beauty and the divine mingled with all that was holy and joyful.

I forget the name of the group that sang the slow moving song. But, I'll never forget how I loved the touch of a special young lady in my arms as we slowly moved on the wooden floor that served as both a dance floor and a gym floor.

We'd touch, hand in hand and arm against arm. No, we'd never do the "grind." That was a dirty type of a dance, where you hardly moved, except to bend the girl backwards while you leaned forward with those private parts coming into closer contact than you ever had experienced before.

I sang Doo Wop as a baritone-bass for my five-man group which once appeared on television. It was at a time that the Righteous Brothers were introducing what they called "Blue-Eyed Soul." We were a bunch of white guys singing like we were black. Yes, we wanted to be as black as the Moonglows, the Spaniels and the Harptones. They were the greatest groups of my generation that spanned the 1950s and 1960s.

We wanted to sing as softly and as rowdy as the wind, be it a smooth caressing version of the "Ten Commandments of Love", or a fast dance song like the one by the Earls.

See if you can remember this one:

> "Re-mem-mem, re-mem-mem-mem-ber oop-shoop
> Re-mem-mem, re-mem-mem-mem-ber oop-shoop
> Re-mem-mem, re-mem-mem-mem-ber oop-shoop then
> Then, remember then . . ."

It was all part of growing up in an urban setting made popular by American Bandstand and some of the greatest disc jockeys this side of Dick Clark's forever youthful-looking face. Hy Lit and Jerry Blavat played the songs and we copied them blowing our harmony on street corners and "under the Boardwalk" and "Up on the Roof."

Whenever I think of music, I'll always think of my Doo Wops days and Doo Wop nights.

Blow brother, blow.

Let the "oohs" and the "aahs" take us all away.

Recalling childhood angels with dirty faces

I CAN THINK OF NO worse place to be than in a church, a temple or a syna-gogue when an unbidden and involuntary giggle would invade my psyche and take control of me. A "giggle," is too mild a word: uncontrollable laughter would rise to the level of guffaws and downright knee-slappers' right at the most somber parts of a religious service.

I noticed it while still in high school and my mother would shake me awake in time to make the 12 o'clock mass, the last one on a Sunday at our parish church. I'd still be half asleep as I snaked my way into St. Ludwig's Catholic Church in Brewerytown, North Philadelphia, just as the choir would finish its first Latin rendition of some hymn. Dipping my hand in a well of liquid, I'd touch my forehead, my chest and both of my shoulders with holy water while seeking a place to stand in the back of the church.

You'd find a group of guys leaning against a marble railing some eight feet across guarding a statute of some saint or other behind it. I didn't know it then, but they were my role models, the older fellows those of us in our mid-teens looked up to. I wanted to be as cool as "Chalky" Thompson who'd sing a mean and raucous rock & roll bass to the Doo Wop song, "Mopity Mope" by The Boss-Tones. To be acknowledged by someone like a Jackie Toy, who'd later become a mentor for me, would simply make my holy day of obligation a *great* day.

We'd all gaze to the front where a priest adorned in his vestments would be making sacrificial offerings on the steps of an altar. We'd barely hear what he said, but knew the responses by heart having served as altar boys while in the church's elementary school.

Someone would whisper something. You wouldn't hear it at first, but you'd see the response and the effect it'd have on the intended listener. "What did he say?" I'd ask and someone would answer, causing the first belly laugh. Old people in pews ten to 15 feet in front of us – those still with good hearing – would turn and give us looks of warning. But it would be too late. One laugh would lead to another. I'd try to swallow the giddiness, but it would only get worse, with me forcing myself to turn away from my fellow blasphemers and seek an out. I'd raise my hands to cover my face, using a prayer-book or one of those weekly church pamphlets to hind behind.

But the laughs would just continue. God-awful laughs would rise up and need to be released as tears would come to my eyes and I'd bend forward pointing my head toward the church floor looking for some miraculous hole to open for me jump into to hide.

It would seem forever before I got control of these involuntary laughs. I'd feel so bad, but also so good, if you know what I mean. There I was in the house of prayer and I'd feel a goodness — a forgiveness — come over me despite my behavior. Was osmosis of some sort taking place? Were the congregations' prayers and meditations getting through to me and the other rowdy sinners in the back?

Maybe. I'd really feel sorry for disturbing anyone during services, but I'd feel uplifted by sharing those stupid happy moments with like-minded persons.

After all these years, I still enjoy a good laugh while acting a little devilish in the presence of a Higher Being. I intend no harm, and I believe whenever two or more are gathered in His Name ". . . there is love . . ." — not to mention a lot of fun.

War stories penetrate a family gathering

THE KNIFE "*BROKE SKIN*" AND went about an inch in to my back.

I felt the pain all the way to the emergency room, believing the knife still lodged there. I could not tell . . . I dare not turn to try to see or touch it.

My brother, Johnny Contos, threw the knife when he thought I cursed at mom. "*It was a butter knife*" he recalls decades later. "*And it fell out before you left the house.*"

Never thought of the incident as a big deal. Neither did Johnny. I remember hearing stories about pop, Achilles Contoveros, who had a similar temper and cut a guy when he felt someone had disrespected mom. He worked as a cook and she, a waitress, had been visiting, when some guy got fresh with her, according to the story. Next thing you know, pop stabbed the guy in his hand with one of those long carving forks. Not sure if both prongs went through the hand.

Unsure if my dad lost his job over the incident. But it was no big deal. Mostly hushed up when someone tried to bring it up at dinner table later.

The knife incident occurred on a holiday when Jimmy Suss, one of my best friends growing up and two years older than me, had called and invited me to a picnic. Got excited at age 13 or 14. Jimmy was cool, in the same grade as Johnny, but he accepted me more as a peer than my brother did. Johnny had to "*watch*" me sometimes, and I didn't like him exerting authority over me. (*Had a dream several months ago . . . saw myself looking up from a hole . . . my brother poked me with a long stick . . . I begged him to stop . . . he wouldn't . . . not until I got out of the hole . . . grabbed the stick and ran after him wanting to kill him with multiple blows to the head.* Woke up and finally understood our relationship as siblings.)

Mom said I couldn't go. That I had to stay at home in our Brewerytown, North Philadelphia, row house. I took a fit, particularly, when she told me to "*Read your book.*"

"*Book Fook,*" I said, rhyming as much as I could, staying a good centimeter away from crossing the line of disrespect. Never did curse mom or pop. Ever.

Johnny was eating breakfast, probably bacon and eggs along with buttered toast. "*Don't you curse at my mother,*" he said with an angry voice, and threatening tone that I still fear today on recalling it from the 60s.

He threw the breakfast knife and it went into my back as I turned to ward off the throw. It penetrated, going into the lower portion where I wear the scar and I cried, not fully understanding what had happened. "*I got a knife in me back,*" went through my mind, as I thought of the Disney movie "Treasure Island" and young Master Hawkins dealing with the likes of Long John Silver's scallywags.

Made no sense. Except it allowed me to escape any thoughts of death. "*. . . got a knife in me back . . .*" was all in play, part of an adventure, an imaginative mind over matter trick that kept me from . . . I don't know . . . going into shock . . . or wanting to retaliate.

Was treated and released from the hospital. Johnny doesn't like it when I bring up the story. But it's all part of our "*colorful*" background. And makes for a war story of sorts to tell at family gatherings. I told you I came from a tough neighborhood. It all started at home.

Secret code broken by number of rings

As KIDS WE HAD SECRET codes that we would send over what the old fashioned telephone system is now. You'd ring twice, hang up, and then call back immediately.

Hearing the signal, my friend would pick up, knowing he was being called by someone other than a bill collector. Or a "*process-server*." I learned to do this while growing up in Brewerytown and continued it following a divorce and working as a newspaper reporter.

I only did it when single, and wanted to duck callers. You see, I was trying to avoid people looking for money. Not that I was a deadbeat. I was just tardy. For instance, I'd let an electric bill go for months without paying it, even though I had the money in the bank. There was just so many more important things to focus on. Money — or paying it out — was not one of them.

I'd brag about a joke I'd pull on my creditors, saying that each month, I write down the name of all of those I owed money, put 'em in a hat, and pull one out. That's the one I'd pay. And if someone would make demands, I'd threaten to take their name out of the hat.

I didn't care that much about credit-rating. I was paying off a car for the three years and lived in an apartment. Wore old clothes, even when dating. Heck, one woman who visited my "*bachelor pad*" in *Pottstown*, PA, swore she'd never get over a pair of loafers I left lying on the living room floor. Looked like they were "*bit*," and had a "*bite mark*." They did. From my dog *Willie*. They were my favorite shoes. His too! Slip-ons with a well-worn smell to 'em. Mighty comfortable though. Sure wish I had them, but my second wife forced me to throw 'em out.

Was I the only one who used the old telephone code with family and friends? This was the days before "*Caller ID*." You couldn't tell who was calling. There was nothing like a "*No Call List*" for which to subscribe. You were at the mercy of *Ma Bell*.

Ring twice, hang up, & call again!

> (*Oops. Forgot. Bell Telephone Company was broken up years ago. It was a monopoly. Had little if any competition, and the federal government forced it to divide into smaller entities. [Talk about a hang up!]*)

Marketing folk would call you at dinner time to sell a "*time-share*" in a condo at some Florida swamp land. You either picked up the phone or let it ring . . . and ring . . . and ring . . . Had no answering machines back then.

Sometimes, I would lie. Outright. Tell someone trying to sell me children's' books that my child recently died, and then choke up, as they try to comfort me. I usually did this while entertaining visitors. I'd use a really great line from a short story called, "*Bartleby, the Scrivener*," by Herman Melville (the "*Moby Dick*" author). "*I prefer not to*," is all I would say in response to whatever they asked of me. "*I prefer not to*." It would drive 'em crazy. They'd ask for a reason and simply get the same reply: "*I prefer not to*." Many would hang up in frustration. I still do this with some political parties seeking money. "*I prefer not to*." "*I prefer not to*." "*I prefer not to . . .*"

Try it! If it doesn't work, just call me. Make sure you ring twice, hang up, and immediately call back, and hang up after three more rings . . . *and I'll let you stay on line to talk to my answering machine after only a short 10 minute wait.*

Hopping trains fools no one but myself

I'LL NEVER HOP A TRAIN again.

I got dragged and nearly fell beneath a train before finally letting go of a freight car's' metal hand holds. Don't know how far my legs scraped and bumped along the wooden beams and fistfuls of rocks strewn from track to track. Don't remember how long I lay on the ground, long after the train rolled by, thanking God for letting such a foolish boy like me to continue to live.

Think I was 12, maybe 13. I remember singing the Gary "*US*" Bonds song "*New Orleans*," as I tried to impress a gang I wanted to join back then. We'd hike through the train tunnel near the Philadelphia Art Museum. We played on the rocks of the museum, in the Fairmount section. We also swam and waded in the fountains along the steps leading up to the museum.

But hopping a train is nothing like scaling the walls to the museum. There's a certain thrill one would get in "*making*" the train, and getting a ride from one place to another. In addition, it proved you were "*tough*" and could hang out with the tough guys.

Had to fight one of them to be accepted. His name was Billy Van Horn. No one won, but because I "*held my own*" with someone two or three years older than myself, I got a reputation for being a fighter. It felt good to get respect. I never got a big head or anything. It just allowed me to be myself and not worry about fitting in. I became *"one"* of the guys, several of whom might be considered *"bad"* but only to *"goody-two-shoes"* who never took chances.

And jumping onto a moving train is chancy, let me tell you. You have to run along and time it just right to grab the *"ladder-like"* bars on the side of a freight car. Once you got a good grip, you'd hop up to the lower rung, placing both feet on the metal, and hold on for dear life as the train picked up speed and you hoped it would slow down when it got to where you wanted to jump off. Don't believe the movies where you see someone jumping from a fast-moving train and walking away unhurt and not a little sore from hitting the ground where rocks and debris lie. I always got hurt if I failed to get my legs moving fast enough while departing from a train.

But I remember *"hanging out"* with Tommy Van Horn, Billy's younger brother, as well as a couple other delinquent types. We were walking on the tracks that paralleled the Schuylkill River from Philadelphia's Boat House Row all the way to East Falls where there was a public swimming pool.

A train came by. No one tried to hop it. It was going too fast. But not too fast for me. Hopping this one would be a challenge, something the guys would talk about and add to the reputation I was developing. That I was a *"little crazy,"* but more importantly, that I had a *"lot of heart."*

I ran with the train. It was going fast. But I grabbed the handles and continue to keep pace step by step and all I had to do was take one or two more steps and jump to get aboard . . . when I stumbled.

Too afraid to let go, I hung on, as the train dragged me, dragged my legs. I thought I would die at the curve that my body somehow would be thrown beneath the train and onto the tracks where metal wheels would run over me. Is this what it'll be like at war when some Viet Cong is shooting at you and you're uncertain of your next move, but know you must take some action for fear no action would be worse?

I "*let go*," figuratively and literally. I let my fate up to God, asking for forgiveness for hanging with the wrong crowd and promised to reform. Van Horn got to me first. He thought I was dead. I had not moved for several long minutes as he ran up to me.

He called my name. I did not respond immediately. Others joined us. Someone touched my back as I lie face down on the side of the tracks. I slowly spoke and assured everyone I had no broken bones or major cuts.

Forgot all about my promise to God later that day when Van Horn recounted my adventures to others, and I sat in silence, smiling and quietly taking in the admiration for such a daring act. *Many years would pass before I could look back and wonder why God protected such a fool like me. And I am ever so grateful.*

Feeling 17 again, despite the aging process

I DON'T FEEL MY AGE nowadays. I know I'm getting older and will soon meet my Maker. But I just can't see myself as a senior citizen, let alone someone who will one day praise the glory of Medicare and the free rides on public transportation in Philadelphia.

To tell you the truth, I feel like I'm seventeen years old again. My body would disagree, but my heart and my mind often see things from that period of time . . . It was a time when I had just graduated high school and the world was my oyster, so to speak.

I remember singing my heart out as did in a Doo Wop group, even though that term did not come into general usage for another generation or so. There's nothing quite like four-part harmony. Today, I settle for singing along with the radio and my old CDs.

I'd still be a virgin, although I'd never admit it to guys I grew up with. I got a reputation to consider, you know. But I'd laugh and joke just to see the young girls smile and laugh along with me!

And I would speed like a demon in my '57 Chevy with no care for the past or the future. I'd burn rubber until Uncle Sam knocked on my door two years later and invited me to a place called Vietnam.

Jacky Toy taught me how to harmonize, He learned it while singing with Joey Oz and Eddie Keller, two "old heads." They sang "Guardian Angels" at the all-black Uptown Theatre for the midnight talent show. I'll never forget it.

Joey Oz (also known as Joseph Osborne) recently cut a new record. (Oops, I should have said "CD.") He plans to send a copy to me and others feeling 17-years-old at heart. His music company is Brewerytown Records. I feel young when I hear the harmony and I want to sing and dance again all night long!

I still flirt with many woman I come into contact with, hoping I'd get lucky. It never worked then, and it doesn't work now, my friend. But, I feel I'm bringing a little joy to members of the opposite sex when I compliment them and get a smile or two. I believe I'm serving a higher purpose when I serve them, if you know what I mean.

My biggest problem, however, is the continued "need for speed." I still race in the car as if I was back in the classic Chevy. I get road rage and completely stressed out unless I leave for my ride extra early and I meditate while driving. I lose patience with other drivers. I lose patience with myself; and wish I could grow out of it.

But if that's the only drawback of feeling like you're 17, I'll take it any old day. I'll grow up someday, but for now I'll enjoy life while still feeling young!

Some lessons go down easier than others

⎯⎯⎯⎯⎯⎯

MY GOD, WHEN WILL THIS pain end? I can't take it anymore. Please, just take it away. Or let me die.

This is the worse day of my life. That will include pain I'll suffer as bombs explode and persons around me later die in Vietnam. At least that will be quick and done with . . . This agony is so *prolonged*. And the worst of it is, I brought it all on myself.

I drank too much. But how was I to know beer and mixed drinks don't really "*mix*?" Pop told my older brother not to mix drinks at a party, but I thought he meant pouring beer, wine and hard liquor into a glass to create a "*Zombie-like*" drink. What does it actually mean? "*Don't mix your drinks?*" Don't drink beer and switch to other alcoholic beverages later? Or don't *mix* anything with Whiskey, Scotch or a Bourbon? Pop drank his "*straight*" or with only a few ice cubes, calling it "*on the rocks.*"

I feel like I'm "*on the rocks.*" Crashed and burning on 'em. Why didn't I listen? Christ, I'm almost 18. Finished high school when I was just 17 and I've been working full-time four months now. Drank beer with the older fellows lots of times. Even got served at the *Big Moose Bar*, 30th and Stiles streets (in *Brewerytown*), when African-American bartenders couldn't tell my age, me, their cross-racial White patron.

And I've been drunk before. Well, a little high, and needed to sleep it off. But never like this. And, here I am. It's not quite 9:30 in the morning. Having to come to work at *Johnson & Prince*, a printing firm at 12th and Samson streets, in *Center City Philadelphia*. I'm a printer, a lithographer who develops negatives via a camera and developing solutions, before "*stripping*" goldenrod sheets. I use an X-Acto knife to cut away paper to expose a negative to high intensity lights. These lights or "*lamps*" will "*burn an image*" onto a metal plate to help produce the printed word — all during this golden age of advertising. (The late 1960s)

I sit on a tall wooden stool, leaning over a table covered by glass. A light shines up from beneath the glass to allow me to see tiny pinholes in the black negative. My job is to cover all those pinhole lights with a black liquid substance.

The light shines *through* me. And *into* me. *Over and below me*, reminding me how I had just struggled with the piercing brightness while getting out of bed a half-hour earlier, making it to work ten minutes late on little more than three hours of sleep.

Lord have mercy on me a sinner.

Don't know what hurts more. The pulsating head or the acid-volcano eruptions in my stomach and esophagus. I wish I was dead. Didn't I just say that? But, wait! Can't die until after collecting the time-and-a-half pay for coming in on a Saturday. I work the second shift. From noon until 9 pm, giving me all the time in the world to party after work. What more could a healthy God-fearing teenager want than to drink long and hearty knowing he could sleep in the next day.

Except for mornings when I'm needed for over-time work. And have to drag myself through a haze of pre-meditated hell. The devil's pre-meditation, knowing he better get me while I'm young and foolish, instead in my middle age when a spiritual awakening will help moderate my drinking habits.

I'll survive this. Like to say it taught me a lesson. But I'll suffer through it a half-dozen more times before realizing that insanity occurs when you expect a different outcome while doing the same thing over and over.

Now, if I could have just treated the stock market and my **401 (k)** the same way, seeing the insanity of it all, I'd be in better shape, sharing a toast with you now.

Getting 'fired' up for singing debut on TV

Mr. JR Johnson fired me when he caught me *"entertaining"* friends at his place of business. The Johnson and Prince printing establishment in Philadelphia.

He waited until the end of the shift Friday, and told me my days (actually, nights) as a stripper were over. I tried to explain, apologize for my actions, but that evening it was to no avail.

It hung over me that weekend. But did little to dim one of the brightest moments of my life.

I performed on television. Harmonized with my singing group on the Super Lou Television Dance Show, as a member of *"The Five Jaunts."* We did two Doo Wop songs that made the girls swoon and the guys snap fingers and sing along. I sang with two other guys from Brewerytown (North Philadelphia), and two from the more affluent Far Northeast Philadelphia, blending a sound that inspired one record producer to offer us a contract, and provide me with a brief period of local fame and notoriety.

We had practiced for nearly a year, and I got fired when members of the group had decided to pay me a surprise visit. They had come *"downtown,"* purchased identical shirts for our TV *"gig,"* and walked into my nearby center city job site to show me the shirts. We were a group, and it was the closest thing we could come up with for a *"costume."*

They bought shirts with collars that stretched on and on. No buttons, just a gaping space at the chest. I'd recall them when watching a *"Seinfeld"* episode, the one with the *"Puffy"* shirts. They were different, but with the same principle. The boss walked in — I had stopped working to try on a shirt — and he saw what must have appeared as me *"goofy off"* on his time. He fired me after my group left the premises.

The following day, we sang without a hitch to loud applaud from a dance crowd at a studio rented by one of the — at that time — new UHF television stations, Channel 29. This was before VCRs were invented. Never made a visual recording, but the girlfriend of our lead singer, his future and still current wife, eventually *"transferred"* a tape-recorded version onto a CD, and surprised each member years later with a version of our own *"Oldies but Goodies."*

But then, when the crowning achievement of my singing career ended that weekend in the late 60s, I had to return to work, and try to get my job back.

I was a stripper. Went to school to learn the trade. Dobbins Technical High School, where I learned offset printing, the fine art of lithography. I would *"strip"* goldenrod sheets of paper to allow light to *"burn"* images onto a metal plate used in the printing process. I developed the negatives, place the goldenrod sheet over the "neg," and use an X-Acto knife to cut the paper, exposing the reverse letters and *"pictures."* We called this work *"stripping,"* a process that printing inventor Guttenberg could be proud to lay claim to.

Got my job *"back."* It seems, that JR's sister had seen the television show and called her older brother. (He was really old, must have been at least 50.) She confirmed what I had told the boss Friday, the night he fired me. When I showed up for work Monday, he called me into his office, told me that I was "*unfired*," and smiled.

Never did sing on TV again. But I still print. One keyboard stroke after another.

Five Jaunts remembered singing Doo Wop

⤌

I CANNOT RECALL THE ONE and only time I saw myself perform on television with my singing group even though it was one of the highlights of my life.

I sang bass for a Doo Wop group in the late 1960s as we appeared on the Super Lou Dance Show. We sang two songs which were recorded by a film crew. The performance was taped in front of a live audience for Channel 29, a UHF Station with its studio at Old York Road in the Philadelphia suburb of Jenkintown. (Philadelphia had three UHF stations – Channels 17, 29 and 48.)

We auditioned for the show's emcee at his Northeast Philadelphia home and he agreed to performance a few weeks later. We purchased matching shirts like the one Seinfeld wore for his television appearance and we practiced two songs from our "Golden Oldies" repertoire.

I remember walking onto the dance floor and staring at the bright lights that lit us up for the camera. My voice was the first one heard because I opened with a bass sound to start the Rock & Roll beat. I was advised later to remove my glasses because the lights shined too bright and the reflection was distracted.

All went well with the show and I'll never forget Super Lou speaking to us at the end, stating my name as the "boom, boom" man! I couldn't smile any brighter than I did at that wonderful moment. We sounded good and I can tell you there is nothing more divine sounding then harmonizing in a group!

We called ourselves The Five Jaunts. The night of our television appearance, we also "appeared" at a party held by Bob Palumbo in his mom's house in the Brewerytown section of Philadelphia. I remember how a cute little redhead kept giving me the eye. I got my very own "groupie" I thought, but failed to get her more interested in a more intimate relationship after the party.

The problem is, however, I cannot for the life of me remember seeing us sing on television. I have no memory whatsoever and I wonder today if I'm experiencing the early stages of Alzheimer's disease. I simply can't recall the television viewing even though I can remember the performance.

It doesn't really matter. I got a recording of that special night when we appeared on television. It still sounds as good today as it did when I was a "yon teenager" and I suppose it always will.

'Five Jaunts' create a life-long harmony

THE BOTTLE OF LISTERINE SPILLED and the car smelled of antiseptic. A 57 Chevy should never suffer such an indignation.

But, I began carrying the bottle in the glove compartment since the singing group took off, and we'd practice mid-way between where three of us lived in Brewerytown, and Greater Northeast Philadelphia, where two other singers called home. It was a courtesy thing, the glass bottle of mouthwash. I'd use it and pass it on to someone who'd laugh, ask privately if their breath smelled, and laugh even more when I'd dead pan them with a Buster Keaton unflinching look and a sorrowful nod "*yes.*"

Loved to sing. No, make that "*harmonize.*" Blend my voice with another even if it was only one person. But, three-part harmony was made to appease the Greek gods, create visions of gentle waterfalls and meadow lands where an imagination could create a shepherd with their flock, whether it was a young David or a Little Boy Blue.

We'd create a beauty to listen to, standing in the second floor landing of an exit to the "*El*" train stop at Bridge and Pratt. Standing on this side of the metal turnstile, passengers exiting the car of an "*Elevated*" train would often slow down. Not out of fear of five tough-looking white teenagers huddling together foot-ball style singing the "*oohs*" and "*aahs,*" as well as the "*doo wops*" the genre of music would be called one day. But out of appreciation for free "*street-corner*" entertainment. Several "*old head*" would stop, snap their fingers, and even join in remembering the words to such standbys as "*Stormy Weather*," "*Zoom, Zoom, Zoom*," and "*Gloria*." Most were black — African-Americans. We had taken their so-called "race music" and tried to mix in a little blue-eyed soul.

"*Practice*" was always fun. Something I'd look forward to as much as I do for group meditation now-a-days. I was instrumental in bringing together part of the group, but our lead singer, Joe Cleary, actually "*formed*" it and built on the rudimentary "*sounds*" I had introduced. Sounds passed down from older fellows, those really "*old heads*" who were in their early 20s. They had me singing baritone with 'em when I was only 14. *And lovin' every minute of it*, with or without a bottle of Listerine. These guys had sung with *Harold Melvin & the Blue Notes*, met groups like the O'Jays and others that would help create what would be known as the "*Philly Sound*," produced by Gamble and Huff. Singing with them was taking part in a legacy of sorts, whether I knew it or not at the time.

And, I'd "*pass on*" what I learned to guys my age, seeking to harmonize after school let out and on weekends, until forming an a cappella group called the "*Five Jaunts*." Sang together for only a year, but felt more like a life-time, as we appeared on television, stage and many a bathroom with good acoustics in the row house of someone throwing a party.

The '57 Chevy is gone. It was more than 10 years old when I bought it for $300 in the late 1960s. Listerine no longer makes a "*glass*" container, but a plastic one. And, the music of yesteryear is just a memory, one I still dream about . . .

Like last night, as I dreamed of coming out of a building, seeing kids gathering together on the pavement, and heard voices blending as one; I approached, listened with my eyes closed, and knew I would always carry that harmony within me . . .

Monkey see, and alas, Monkey will do

The fool showed up uninvited to the beach house in Wildwood, NJ, and created a mess good folk hardly talk about now-a-days. He sat "Indian-style" on the living room rug with Billy Kane, both about the same age, 18 to 19. There were two or three other guys drinking beer as Billy passed 'em around. And then Kane "barfed" on the fool. Threw up onto the fool's bare legs uncovered by the summer shorts he wore. "Kanie," as we called the one who "likes his brew," smiled a devilishly Irish grin, before offering a fake apology. The fool said nothing. We thought he would take offense by Kanie's antics, something he had done for laughs before among those who liked his raunchy sense of humor.

LIKE THE TIME KANIE WAS auditioning to perform on television with his singing group, "The Five Jaunts," an a cappella group that entertained "Under the Boardwalk" and "Up on the Roof" near the row houses back home in Brewerytown, a working class section of North Philadelphia. Kanie let loose with a stinker. I mean, it was so bad, the statue of William Penn standing atop City Hall turned and faced another direction. One by one, each singing group member began to notice.

"Ew," the first tenor, Jimmy Hubmaster said, with nose scrunched up making the universal expression something smelled bad. Carl Disler, our baritone, was more stoic-looking, but did glance in Kanie's direction. The noxious fume finally hit me, and I stopped singing bass altogether, backing away from the ripe one's air space. Joe Cleary, the lead singer, yelled at us for fooling around but laughed when we explained what happened.

Trouble is, Kanie had little control over the expulsion. It was one of those you really should "never trust," as Jack Nicholson said in the movie, the "Bucket List." He let out a "wet one," moments before we were to meet in the house of Super Lou, a local disc jockey, who would decide whether we were gifted enough to appear on his weekly teenage dance show on that newly created UHF station, Channel 29, owned by Taft Broadcasting.

The smell lingered with Kane as Super Lou answered the knock at his Greater Northeast Philadelphia home, introducing us individually to his wife before being escorted into the kitchen. Did he move away from the group because of Kanie's aroma? Could not tell, but hoped Lou would remain far enough "downwind "to enjoy the singing without noticing any unfavorable fragrances. We sang two songs, both of which we practiced for nearly a year on street corners and in Kanie's cellar at 28th and Poplar.

Super Lou liked us. Gave us the "okay" and we performed a week or two later, with nary a hint that he picked up on Kane's calling card.

The fool back in Wildwood said nothing about Kanie's behavior, but went into the bathroom, closed the door and apparently cleaned off the mess. He returned with a wad of toilet paper in his hand. Taking aim at Kanie, he threw its contents at the unapologetic and still smiling Kanie. It was "Scota." Landed on Kanie's bare chest and fell to the floor where he still held his beer can. Kanie looked down, gathered up the projectile, and threw it back, missing the fool and hitting another beer swiller. All hell broke loose, as crap got tossed throughout the room, landing on furniture, rugs and the drapes. Not sure how it ended up on the front screen door, but the "shit hit the fan," so to speak when Monica, the most prim and proper (can anyone say "tight" as in "up-tight") person I've even known, opened the door, asking about the substance clinging to the screen, when something flew her way, and she screamed upon recognizing it.

The fool left, and was not seen by Kanie and the gang for more than three decades. I think about him when I marvel at how far I've progressed, and how great humans have climbed the evolutionary ladder. Actually, we had nowhere to go but up, from when a

Values don't change in impermanent world

I was 18 when I asked Janet to marry me, and she turned my request down flat. We were never romantically involved, even though I'm sure a mutual love would have grown out of our teenage friendship.

Janet got pregnant. She felt uncertain about her future. And whether the boy she had dated the past year would share the responsibility a new-born would require. What should have been a glorious time in her life, became one filled with questions, anxiety and a concern for what tomorrow would bring. This was the 1960s, the age of Free Love. A period that would soon usher in Women's' Liberation and a freedom to experiment with all kinds of lifestyles, including single parenthood.

But, we grew up in a working class neighborhood that held other values, and I felt Janet was too nice a person to be labelled an *"unwed"* mother, and the connotations that went with it, if I could have anything to do with it.

That's when I told her I'd marry her and help raise the child. I meant it. You see, Janet had become what I later would call my *"confidante,"* a person I felt comfortable with sharing my every thought about life and love. We'd commiserate about our mutual struggles, me with my girlfriend, Peggy McPeake, and her with the only person I knew who — up until the time I turned 19 –had ever attended a college, a brilliant fellow who was articulate and gifted.

He turned me on to a book involving a wizard and a rabbit-like creature called a "*Hobbit*," and opened me to a life full of imagination and wonder. Reading became a pleasure as I developed new ideas for my dreams, new forms of hope in the world.

Don't need a pat on the back for acting noble or anything. I just thought that marrying Janet would be the right thing to do. And even now, with all the so-called knowledge I've gained over the years, I still think it would have worked.

Janet married the fellow, raised the child, and eventually divorced. I lost track of her when drafted into the army, served in Vietnam and went through my own marriages and divorce.

But, I recalled this marriage proposal after observing my son and his relationship with girls. He doesn't have a date for the prom yet, and I suggested the name of one of his friends. "*She's got a boyfriend*," he said. "*So what?*" I said, thinking that she was "*only a kid*" whose teenage feelings cannot possibly be as deep and committed as that of an older person, an adult.

And then it hit me. My son holds the same values I had at his age. Values that haven't been tested to see if they are still held as dear to me today as they were years ago.

My son helped me realize how important these values still were when he told me how he "*honored*" the boyfriend/girlfriend relationship. And he would probably offer to help out a friend the same way I did when I was his age. It made me proud to be his dad. Proud to know somethings may not change despite all the impermanence around us.

Are you the one from a path not taken?

~&~

WHY ARE YOU FOLLOWING ME?

Who are you, and where do you come from, my friend who shadows me? Silently, you visit this site, watching, and not saying a word, leaving hardly a trace, except for the Internet "name" containing the initials, "MC." I welcome you. I believe you mean no harm. And I like to think I know who you really are.

"MC" could be a disguise for the girl I thought I'd eventually marry, Peggy McPeake. Her Baptismal name was "Margaret." "MC" could stand for the "Mc" in McPeake.

Is it you?

We dated off and on for five years, starting April 11, 1963. I had that precise moment engraved in one of the rings I gave you. No, not my high school ring from Dobbins Technical High School, from the North Philadelphia neighborhood called "Swampoodle." It might have been the black pearl I surprised you with as a ring on your sweet 16th birthday.

We had been "broken up" and were "seeing" others a good six months before I was drafted into the US army. Was in the military a year and a half when I was devastated upon hearing the news from my mother on a call I made from Ft. Polk,

Louisiana, to Pennsylvania. "Did you hear that Peggy got married?" I remember the words as if they were spoken yesterday.

You probably never knew it, but my world "shifted" on learning about your wedding. I felt the bottom of my very existence had fallen through. I did not know it, until that moment, how much I had depended on you being "there" for me. There back home, when I really did not have any good basis on which to believe you would be there. Other than, I don't know, a hope you'd always be there; always be the "stability" in my life.

Someone told me that you got pregnant, had to get married. Some Armenian fellow who ran a pizza store. When I saw you some 10 years later, divorced from my first marriage, to a young woman I met in Mamou, Louisiana, shortly after your marriage, I could not tell you how crushed I felt. How I took a train home, saw my reflection in the window and wondered for the first, but not the last, "Who Am I?" Definitely not the man to "live happily ever after" with you, Peggy. I never cried over it. But, deep inside I mourned for who we were, the childhood sweethearts, the senior prom dates. The innocent, even virgin, boy and girl that we cherished.

Did your mother, Mary, tell you I came to see you while on leave as a second lieutenant? "How is she?" I asked as she opened the door to your row house on Poplar Street in our old neighborhood, Brewerytown. "Fine, the baby's fine," she said, directing my attention away from you and toward your new family member, a baby girl. I thought I was going to lose it then. I had just turned 21 a few weeks earlier. At that precise moment, I felt more like 61. My life seemingly over.

"OK," I said, turning away to prevent anyone from seeing me full in the face. Did not know if I'd be able to control what I was feeling. "Tell here I said 'hi,'" I think I said while walking down the steps and away from a "road not taken."

What would it have been like? A life together. More predictable? Perhaps. More grounded? Probably. But this allowed both of us to fly in a different direction, one that, in the words of the poet describing a road not taken, "has made all the difference."

(See Part II Next)

Mc572 – who are you & how can we talk?

WHO ARE YOU MY MYSTERIOUS stranger? The only information I got from your e-mail contact was an address that took me nowhere. It was "Mc572".

I have no idea how to confirm who you are, my mysterious visitor. It has haunted me for weeks and weeks and I just had to say something about it.

Who are you? The title "Mc572" just doesn't cut it. Please let me know who you really are. I've seen you at my site for months. You visit almost every day, but have not left a word or any message to indicate what your interest might be. I have tried, but have been unable to reach you, to determine if you're a *friend* or a *foe*.

I joined Yahoo and a bunch of other forums like Twitter, Face Book and My Space in hopes of contacting you. But, lacking any computer savvy, I couldn't trace you through Microsoft or Google using this "call sign."

So, I'm going to decide right here and now that you are a *friend*. Perhaps, an old *girlfriend*. I hope you're not the first one I was "*fixed up*" with on an after-noon "*blind date*." We had nothing in common. I was a street urchin, well, a city boy, actually, and you were from the "*proverbial*" other side of the tracks, the suburbs, from a middle class family that rolled up their windows, locked all their car doors, and speeded up when driving through my neighborhood of Brewerytown.

Maybe you're "*Maureen,*" that wonderful girl who kept looking at me from the movie theater I visited in Kensington, another tough neighborhood in North Philadelphia. I loved how you would turn your head and look in my direction. I like to think you were looking at me. I was *hoping* you'd look at me. I liked you immediately, and for the first time in my life — at age 12 — I felt I understood "*love at first sight.*" I never saw you after we exchanged first names, and shyly promised each other that we'd meet again. "*See you,*" I said finding the courage to look you in the eye. "I'll see you too," you replied, turning your body a little awkwardly as you clutched your hands in front of you. "*Right here, here at the movies?*" "*Yeah, right here.*"

I never did make it back to the theater.

Did you?

LSD truthfulness speaks to past love lost

"I love Peggy," I opened up and whispered to the girl whose heart I believe I had just broken.

"I didn't mean to hurt you. I just thought you needed to know, that's all," I continued.

THE GIRL, WHOSE NAME WAS Peaches, said nothing as we sat on the floor of the vestibule in her Fairmount home. I saw her eyes water up and I wanted to cry myself. We had dated for two to three months and visited each other's house, after introducing each of us to our families. We never went steady, but were good friends who learned so much exploring the times we'd spend together alone.

"I still love her" I added, unable to look at Peaches.

"I guess I never stopped loving her, if you want to know the truth."

Peaches was a dark-haired girl of 18. I was just a year older when we started to share such intimate moments. She was Peggy's best friend in high school and knew her as much as anybody did, I recalled. I would argue and break up with Peggy, but we'd always got back together every single time. Peaches knew that when we first started dated.

"I should have been honest with you. I wouldn't hurt you for any-thing. I liked you, I still like you.

But I don't love you. I love Peggy, and I guess I always will."

Looking back, I now know what might have caused me to speak this way to that young woman. I had dropped a tab of acid earlier in the evening and was under the influence of drug I knew next to nothing about!

I was on a trip, an acid trip that one of my old singing buddies gave to me as he escorted me as a guide in the summer of 1968.

Acid is lysergic acid diethylamide, also known as <u>LSD</u> for those unfamiliar with the terminology from the 1960s. Who knew that night that my neighborhood friends in North Philadelphia would hold a surprise going away party for me and my good friend Carl Disler. We both got drafted and were leaving the next day. We sang in our Doo Wop street corner harmony group and would get through boot camp in Fort Bragg, North Carolina, together, and somehow reunite in Fort Polk, Louisiana years later with him returning from Vietnam and me leaving for the war zone following jump school and training to become an officer.

But taking acid was not what it was cracked up to be. I knew it could lead to a higher level of thinking and feeling. I read books suggested by Timothy Leary in the tumultuous 60s. But I didn't foresee that it would work as a truth serum, forcing me to admit to a young woman I briefly dated that I was still in love with my high school sweetheart on the eve of getting drafted and sent into the Vietnam War.

I never did get back together with my high school sweetheart. She married another and so did I. Even when we got back together some ten years after our mutual divorces, it just wasn't the same.

Still, I'll never forget the love I felt for Peggy McPeake that evening in the early days of June in 1968. I remember it today as if it was yesterday.

Or am I just having another one of those LSD flashbacks?

Thanks for a Path that Preserved my Life

EVER WONDER WHAT LIFE WOULD have been like if you made different choices years earlier?

I was 19 when I felt "*separated*" from most of the people I hung out with and called friends. I wanted to be so much like them; not to care about such things as "*love*," "*compassion*," other people's "*feelings*." That was "*sissy*" stuff; stuff that only a "*wuss*" would think about is what I was told. I saw these aspects of myself as a sign of "*weakness*."

Looking back, I now see they gave me a strength, a real "*life-preserver*," and in some cases, a bullet-proof vest. You see, the neighborhood in which I grew up — Brewerytown (small section of North Philly) — was tough. Some friends never made it beyond the age of 30. Others who feared the living of day-to-day, took their own lives before reaching 40. And of course, drugs — which most of us experimented with — sucked the marrow right out of some of the best of us, leaving nothing but the legacy of a lost life behind.

Bobby Mendel was one of those first killed while in his early 20s. A year younger than me, he was a "*late bloomer*," not dating until well toward the end of high school, I seem to recall. He married a lovely young girl from outside of the neighborhood. He was shot by next-door neighbor while defending her honor during an argument outside their home. The shooters went to jail. I lost track of their whereabouts.

"*Big Dave*," a fellow from the bordering neighborhood, Fairmount, was not as lucky. Someone killed him in what we later have named a "*drive-by*" shooting. Never did hear of any arrests. Another young man (maybe 19), whom I only knew as "*Rebel*," died from a broken neck when he dove into shallow water while trespassing at a rock quarry near Conshohocken with other kids from the neighborhood. They could not see the bottom, eyewitnesses said, because the water was so dirty.

Two guys who sang first tenor in singing groups in which I had harmonized may have ended up taking their own lives. *Mikey Dugan*, a fellow who helped get me my first job as a messenger boy at 15, was said to have overdosed following what friends say was a deep depression. He came from a rough family. Brother, *Dusty Dugan*, did "*state*" time for some assault or another. *Moose" Moran*, who also sang with a clear falsetto voice, was rumored to have shot himself near the 29th Street Bridge that separated Brewerytown and Fairmount.

Others died way too early. *Tommy Humphreys*, who fathered a child with one of the 15-year-old girls who "*hung* "out with us, is said to have succumbed to drugs. He chose a hard life, one which contributed greatly to his early demise. I still think of *Connie Magee* birthing their child and having to enter adulthood earlier than the rest of us.

One of the saddest deaths I had to accept involved *Pat Lawn*, clearly the most beautiful girl who hung at *29th and Poplar Streets*. She was the ideal teenager: pretty, soft-spoken, always appearing as a real lady. She also could dance and sing! She would often harmonize with us guys, filling in with the high parts. You knew she came from a good family and that if anyone would make it out of the neighborhood in one piece, it was going to be her. She was loved by many of the guys from my "*crowd.*" *Johnny Keller*, whose kidney failed him before turning 21 and who lived beyond the 20 years doctors gave him to last following a transplant from his brother, Edward, was smitten by her. He carried that with him 'til the day he died. My best friend. Never marrying. Dying before I had a chance to tell him how much he meant to me. To all of us.

Jimmy Suss loved *Pat*, too. He ended up marrying her. But split as problems developed. Some may have involved drugs. Lots of drugs that Pat got drawn to years after breaking up with Jim.

Pat Lawn died from an overdose, taking a little part of all of us who knew her.

Well, I have a lot to be thankful for this November, 2009. Hope I can carry that feeling over to the holidays, Thanksgiving and all. I could have chosen a different path than the one I walk today. I am thankful for lasting this far on the Journey.

III Miscellaneous Memories

Like to change history? Try writing it

How'd you like to go back in time and correct mistakes made in the past? No, you couldn't go back to the moment before you were conceived, or any other time in your far distant past. Go back to more recent moments – say in the past 10 to 30 years or so — when you believed you knew so much about life and how to live it without doing harm to others.

I made some poor decisions as a story-teller, writing things I never should have revealed and sharing thoughts that served no purpose than to make me look good at the expense of someone else. I regret it, and want to tell the world that I am sorry. Better, yet, I can do something about it. When you create stories you have the advantage of controlling them. They spring forth from a writer's mind and somehow appear on canvas in attempts by an author to share some "thing" with another person you hope would take the time to read it. There are as many topics to write about as there are people in the world, but I always believed the best were the more authentic ones. I tried to write authentically, sharing how I felt in a given situation or reflections of a past occurrence.

To make it more "real," I kept the actual names of people intact. Why would someone do such an insane thing? Particularly, someone who professes to have a few smarts?

I can only say that I've worked as a journalist, and, except for some fanciful "creative writing" which is more like fiction than non-fiction, I've tried to stay true to the facts. I wanted to share my reality with others and I believed the best way that I could stay true, was to *name the names* of people.

In the back of my mind, I wanted to preserve something for history. I'm serious. When I studied American history in graduate school, I found that "social history" was sorely lacking. We know history from what is called a "great man" point of view -- that is, from people like a George Washington, a Frederick Douglas, and a Susan B. Anthony. We learn of "great" moments they participated in and helped to shape. But what about the nitty-gritty moments, those that occupy the majority of our daily lives? The best social history, I believe, was presented by Ken Burns in his Civil War series for PBS. In between the battles, he brought people to life through the journals of soldiers facing everyday challenges, be it the lack of meat in their daily rations, or their plans for farming upon discharge from military service. It is their story that moved me. It is what I wanted to give to another generation who'd want to read about some first generation Greek American kid growing up in a tough section of an industrial city in the mid to later part of the 20th century.

So what does this have to do with correcting past mistakes? I can alter what I wrote, and take out any and all stories where I said something in haste that might have offended someone. No, I won't change my dislike for certain judges in Philadelphia Common Pleas Court or the ill will I still hold for a superior officer whose own men tried to frag him while in Vietnam. I'll withhold the last name of the nun who knocked me down the steps. I'll alter the names of the girls I "crushed on" during my teenage years. I'll remove derogatory remarks of non-public figures and erase anything bad said about anyone whose child or loved one would not feel good in reading about him or her once they passed away.

I owe it to some future researcher not to think less of someone of whom I never should have written something unfair about to begin with. It'll still be the truth, but it will be written with something closer to what may be called "right speech."

'Singer of Truth' is Contoveros' Aspiration

THE WORD, "*CONTOVEROS*" IN LATIN means "*Singer of Truth.*" I didn't know that as a child. It was my father's real last name. Someone at Ellis Island shortened it to "Contos." One of my wives once told me that the new word means "Short."

I'm five-foot, six inches tall on my best days, and I don't like to be reminded that I am considered short by most people. Randy Newman, the singer, must have had me in mind when he wrote and sang his song called "Short People." I didn't mind, however. Napoleon was short. So was Jimmy Cagney, the actor. I read that St. Francis of Assisi was not even five-foot-two inches!

And if you can believe the latest research done of what Jesus might have looked like, scientists will tell you that the Savior was only five-foot three inches, or thereabouts.

Enough of the short stuff. I have taken to my father's name, Contoveros, like the proverbial fish out of water, water from the Aegean Sea, to be exact. That's where his home was in a small Greek island named Nysiros.

I started to use the designation when I was painting. I worked with ceramics and then drew and painted a few images at some classes I took. It felt comfortable to carve it on the bottom of the porcelain jar or vase. "Contoveros" looked good at the bottom of the paintings, several of which I framed and are hanging in my living room.

But it was in writing a Blog of that name that Contoveros really took over my psyche. Since day one in October of 2009, I have tried to share the truth that I felt. It comes through meditation and silence when I commune with my muse of the divine spirit that seems to call from within.

If I listen close enough, I can hear the whispers, the soft sounds and words of wisdom that a Higher Force wants me to put onto a computer screen. I feel honored to be such a conduit. Even when my lower self, you know — that ego self — disagrees sometimes, I still let it pour onto the page. I apologize ahead of time for any misunderstandings my words might create. That is not my intent.

But maybe the misunderstanding is what you and I need some time to get our thoughts and feelings straightened out.

I don't know. I'm just a reporter, a messenger who is trying to sing the truth as he feels it.

Dance with Achilles Contoveros again

"To Dance With My Father Again."

WHAT I WOULDN'T GIVE, TO dance with my father again. Or, more likely, watch others — what seemed like the whole Greek nation — dance with him. My father was a dashing man on his feet. Could pass for the brother of the actor Errol Flynn, always taking the lead for what I called the "Greek Snake Dance."

He'd whip out a white handkerchief and get another to hold on, as he swept across a dance floor or the living room where guests would pull furniture out of the way and put the bouzouki music on an old record player. Soon, others would be on their feet, hurrying to get in line, as "Pop" — as we called him — would weave his way this way and that, occasionally throwing one leg into the air and slowly moving it in a wide arc before gliding it back to the floor, to he'd delight of us clapping in the audiences and shouting "*Whoopa!!*"

He'd hit the floor with such a thud, you'd think someone had gotten shot. But the crashing sound was all part of the dance, and he'd expertly (and art-fully) knock the floor at the right moment which was any moment his internal dance steps would take him. I'd join in years later, always toward the end or the middle of the line. Only the best dancers seemed to get toward the front. When one lead dancer would tire, the next would take his place leading us in that serpentine manner winding around one way and then the other.

Pop, who left his home of *Nysiros, Greece* at age 15, would never tire. Either that, or he hid it well.

Even into his mid-70s, people would still urge him to take to the floor. These would be other young men, now older, who remembered my father's glory days on the dance floor. I heard the dance may have originated as a *"warriors"* performance, in attempts by the ancients to showcase the best of Greek's fighting elite. You know, from the stories of *Helen of Troy* and the *Trojan horse*.

Who best to lead them than one named *Achilles.*

Achilles Contoveros.

Love you pop.

To Dance With My Father Again. *What a joy it would be!*

Nysiros holds secrets of life and death

I'll never know what drove Anthoula to take her own life.

A young woman, she's rumored to have stood on the balcony of her family home facing the Aegean Sea, and, gazing into the water, she poured flammable liquid on herself. Some say she waited until the man she loved appeared in a boat making its way into the harbor of the Village of Pali, on the Island of Nysiros, Greece, before she struck the match.

And then, she lit up. Became one with fire, suffering excruciating pain until shock or some other part of the immune system "*took pity on her*" and removed all consciousness. She died. No letter found. No reason given; no legacy to pass on to generations like mine that want to know more of its heritage. The good . . . and the bad.

My Cousin, George, recently told me our Aunt Anthoula ended her life out of "*Love*." That she wanted to make her boyfriend "*jealous*."

I didn't buy it. Our aunt's final movements on this earth were but an act of desperation, a reaching out when all reason for living proved futile. Perhaps even painful. But I said nothing to the senior member of the Contoveros clan. That's the tradition among Greeks. Defer to your elders.

Anthoula was in her mid-20s, the youngest of eight children my Greek grand-parents had raised. George Contoveros was my grandfather. His father was Achilles. I know this, only because Greeks "*from the Old Country*" named the first-born male after the grandfather. My oldest brother was named George, my father, Achilles. The older Achilles, my great-grandfather and his brother, Paul, had 26 children between the two of them, according to Cousin George Contoveros, who was born on the island before his immediate family immi-grated to America, settling in Queens, New York.

The tragedy took place after my father had left the island at age 15, never hav-ing known his younger sister, Anthoula. He returned only once, some 5o years later. His mother and father had passed on, and the property left to him ended up in someone else's hands.

Nysiros was formed from an eruption of the earth some 160,000 years ago, according to scientists studying the Greek island. It is within what is called the Dodecanese archipelago, situated south of Kos. Today, no more than 1,000 souls occupy the island.

> "*Nysiros island is a remnant of a prehistoric volcanic field from which the largest eruption in the eastern Mediterranean (Kos plateau tuff) devas-tated the entire Dodecanese islands,*" according to Wikipedia. "*Although the last magmatic volcanic activity on Nysiros dates back at least 25,000 years, the present . . . activity encompasses high seismic unrest . . . Violent earthquakes and steam blasts accompanied the most recent eruptions in 1871-1873 and 1887 and left large crater holes behind. In 1996 and 1997 seismic activity started with earthquakes of magnitudes up to 5.5.*"

An "*earthquake*" on a different scale shook my ancestors when they discovered what Anthoula had done. I can only imagine the crying and wailing of the old Greek women, the stoic painful looks the men shared — all wondering if there was anything anyone could have done to prevent such a travesty.

And then, the cover-up. How it was hushed up. Never spoken of in the New World. Unless . . . or until . . . someone poked a skeleton in the closet, wanting to shed light on the darkness.

Anthoula. May you rest in Peace! And may your soul find the loving and compassionate connection you felt was missing years ago.

Your fond nephew, *Michael J*

A Hagel/Westergom union fits my granny

THE ONLY GRANDFATHER I EVER knew was a hobo.

He rode the rails from East to West Coast, eating chicken and other foods he'd *"gather"* during the years crossing this great land, even ending up in Alaska, where he prospected for gold.

He was a Hagel, Peter Hagel. The second one my *"mother's mother"* had married. Both were from Hungary. Not sure of the town. While Grandpa was the second Hagel to marry Grandma Anna, he was third in line to sire children, after my biological grandfather produced four children with my Granny, and Hagel's older brother three.

And what about that Westergom fellow? He was possibly from Canada. With another wife he never revealed to the one and only grandmom I ever knew. (The Greek side doesn't count. Achilles Contoveros, my father, sired me in his 50s long after emigrating at age 15 from Greece. His parents passed before I knew much about 'em or got a chance to travel to the Greek *"homeland."*)

Step-grandfather Hagel was a bum. He told my cousin, Rosemarie Lieb, why he asked grandmom to marry him when she already had seven children. *"I always believed it best to marry a woman with kids who would look after her . . . and me,"* he told Rosemarie sometime during the Eisenhower years.

Each summer, Hagel would leave the *"comfort* "of his home in the Mays Landing, NJ, to sleep in his *"hobo* shack." A dilapidated one story, one-room structure more like a shed than a residence. Most times, he'd sleep in the woods under the stars, where I guess he was comfortable.

Got shanghaied in San Francisco, according to Rosemarie. Was drinking with some friends when he passed out, having been drugged. They woke up on a ship miles away from the shore. *"There was nowhere to go,"* Hagel told Rose and other grandkids who got him talking in between puffs of a pipe that will always remind me of a tobacco-smoking', stinking' old man. (Always smelled of tobacco. Even when dressed up with a white shirt and not smoking!)

Hagel remained with the ship two years. Went to Alaska. Panned for gold there. Took part in the *"gold rush"* of the Klondike around 1898, according to Rosemarie. No, he was nowhere near San Francisco when the Earthquake struck in 1906, although he did have friends there at the time, someone said.

Learned he was a hobo at a family reunion the past weekend. Met a son of my cousin, Tom Westergom, at the gathering. Hope he'll research the history of my other grandfather, his great-grandfather. Grandpa Westergom had fathered two sons and two daughters before he left the New Jersey *"farm,"* making my grandmom a single parent who made ends meet by travelling to nearby Atlantic City to sell flowers, eggs and crafts she made at the nearby Hamilton Township home.

She learned that Westergom was married with a wife in one of the *"provinces"* of Canada. Kicked him out upon returning to his *"second"* family. Westergom reportedly got a rifle, entered the home and threatened to kill everyone, including my mother, also named Anne, before my Uncle Rudy got him out of the house and into the Trenton, NJ, State Prison for the Criminally Insane, where he lived until his death in 1952. There's a gravestone for him, my Uncle Joe told us years ago when he was still living, having gone to Trenton to get more information but got stonewalled by such a tight-lipped institution.

Wish I had more, but a lot of facts have been hushed up. I always knew grandmom was a pioneer in her day. Never knew how strong a lady she must have been to raise eight kids while being a widow at one time, *"marrying"* a bigamist next, then finding a life-long companion in a hobo.

God Bless 'em all. But you in particular, Grandmom.

Goin' to farm; pick blueberries barefooted

COUSIN ROSEMARIE LIEB, YOU OPENED my heart to something I closed years ago.

Not ready to look inside. Almost, but not just yet.

Your words touched me with a warmth I haven't felt in a long time. They caressed me, and I liken it to a mother's love and pride I couldn't handle at the family reunion last Saturday.

"He wrote speeches for the governor," I heard you whisper to our Cousin John Westergom of whom I have not spoken more than 20 words the past 40 years. I detected a hint of, I don't know, admiration or acknowledgement of an achievement I don't normally dwell on, one I almost forgot. You spoke of something I had tried to forget. My past.

Don't want to look at it. Or focus on it, the so-called achievements, that is. My future's going to be so much brighter. The best years of my life are still ahead. Don't want to sit on my laurels as if Life has passed me by, following a *"retirement"* of sorts with this PTSD disability. I still hope to do so much more and give plenty of myself to humanity, if only in some humble way.

You reminded me of something my mother might have said with pride . . . that her son, Michael J Contos, had gotten a Finnegan Fellowship to study state government in Pennsylvania, thereby insuring a dinner at an awards' banquet with then PA Governor Milton J Shapp. I had studied journalism at the Community College of Delaware County, and was placed in the *"public relations"* division of Penn DOT, the state department of transportation, where I wrote a speech for the governor, several press releases and provided the *"voice over"* for a television newscast introducing new buses that *"kneeled"* to let persons with wheel-chairs enter public transit buses. *"This is Michael Contos, WGOL, Harrisburg,"* I said in my one and only broadcast news report.

It was an achievement, writing for the governor. He used the speech verbatim and I made copies for my resume of *"news clippings."* Never did get a copy of the voice-over. The VCR was not in wide use — if in use at all — in the early '70s.

I wanted to tell you *"it was no big deal."* The kid from a tough Philadelphia neighborhood, Brewerytown, made good, despite his working class roots. You see, I simply dug out a copy of an earlier speech the governor had given, brought it up to date, and put a new spin to it by adding a few of my words that *"Democrats and Republicans alike will join in the celebration"* for the construction feat. Also wanted to tell you I wrote a fictional short story that summer, two years out of Vietnam. The writing got a second place award in an Altoona, PA, contest. (Again, no *"biggie,"* even though it got coverage at Temple University when a teacher published the news in the schools *"house organ."* That's newspaper jargon for a company-operated newsletter.)

You're the only one of my extended family I feel such a *"motherly"* connection with, if that is the right word for it. The type of connection I denied myself growing up, for fear of resting before I could reach some goal, some summit I wanted to ascend to prove I was . . . worthy . . . as a person . . . as a man.

I missed out. Stayed focused too much and too long on nothing but achievements. Now, I want to share those stories I minimized in the past; didn't want anyone to think I got a *"big head."* Still don't, and that's one reason why I've been reluctant to share. Afraid I'll see how unimportant it really was . . . that I was just chasing windmills, if you know what I mean.

Want to visit the farm where Aunt Betty and Uncle Lenny showed us so much love; want to walk barefoot in the sandy roads leading to nearby Atlantic City. And pick lots of blueberries until the proverbial cows come home. Thanks for keeping the light on for this drifter, this black sheep of the family. Hope there's still time enough for us . . .

Police nab attention wherever one roams

I SAW A POLICE VAN and immediately slowed down while driving this morning.

I do it all the time, even if I'm well within the speed limit. Habit, I guess. Always feel that I've done something wrong. Guilt seems to rise to the surface whenever I see police.

It can happen in a restaurant. I could be clean as a whistle. (By the way, what does that really mean? A lack of spittle in the whistle? Then it would be "*dry*" as a whistle, right?) I mean, I could be holding nothing — nothing that could even vaguely resemble contraband –no drugs, no weapons, not even an impure thought or desire. And here it comes, a big: "*uh, oh, what did I do now?*"

Is it simply human nature? Perhaps a trace of left-over "*Original Sin*" that nuns used to ram down some of our Catholic-growing-up throats?

Or, are we really still rebels deep inside; wanting to live our lives outside the box, have fewer restraints, fewer "*shall-nots.*" Remember, there were more than 10 Commandments presented by God to Moses. He ended up chiseling just the first ten into stone for the Israelites. You look at a Bible and I think you may find dozens, if not hundreds, of more orders given to the "*Chosen People*" from on High.

Police represent authority. We gladly grant them that for our own protection, and we praise the men and women who give us their all through their career choices. At least, I have grown to feel this way.

Yet, I remember a time growing up and fearing the police who sometimes went beyond the law to enforce the law. Particularly, against us *"corner loungers,"* the kids that didn't disperse as quickly as a rookie cop may have liked; or the ones that couldn't keep their mouths shut and had to say something that got us all in trouble with the police. When a cop couldn't figure who broke *"his"* law, then we all got blamed for doing it.

Still, you could have grown up with no juvenile delinquents in your block or town. You could be the most law-abiding youth ever to be raised in these United States of America. I bet you still get a slight twinge when you see police, a twinge that at least one, or perhaps both, of your parents instilled in you while correcting some early wayward action. Admit it.

And that's okay.

I think it has to do with the child in us. The child that knows perfection doesn't exist, and that we all fall short of somebody's rule. Police become a reminder that we are still trying to improve our lot, and there will be failings; we'll always make some mistakes and ignorance of the law will never be a valid defense.

I guess I'll take comfort the next time I feel like *"ducking"* upon seeing the *"Man."* (Philadelphia lingo for the police.) They'll be a reminder that I am only human, mistake prone, and how I need to keep *"practicing"* if I ever want to come close to perfection.

Another thought. Do you think Jesus or Buddha ever had a *"twinge"* when seeing authority? Christ never had a liquor license for changing water into something more *"libations"* for his mother, did he? And what ordinance do you think Buddha sidestepped when seeking alms outside village gates? Both spoke to large assemblies with no prior government permits. And both preached about a *"Higher Authority,"* that required no permission to leave a physical state to visit a spiritual one: "*Heaven*" in one language, "*Nirvana*" in another. You could skip the visas or passports when you traveled "*within*," they might have told their followers.

Don't feel as bad about the police now. It's always good to look at law from a historic, spiritual perspective, doesn't it, my "*law-abiding*" friend?

Universe brings music 'Homeward Bound'

I SAW THE SINGER AND songwriter Paul Simon last night and he's *"still crazy after all these years."*

He appeared at the Mann Center for the Performing Arts in Philadelphia to a sold-out crowd of tens of thousands. I got to see him through a friend who got tickets when one of her friends recently had surgery and could not attend. She made the tickets available the morning of the event.

I cried tears of and joy and heartfelt remembrance when the singer offered his final song on stage. It transported me back some forty years and I felt so much compassion for the world that has had to get along without his voice these many years

"The Sounds of Silence" played through me as I recalled watching the movie "The Graduate" with Dustin Hoffman as a 19-year-old candidate in the US Army's Officers Candidate School in Fort Benning, Georgia. It was but a year before being shipped to Vietnam.

It struck the marrow of me then and still does whenever I hear it whether it be live with him playing one of his many guitars on stage, or when hearing it over the radio, an old record player or from a CD.

It was only the second concert I ever attended. The first was at the other "Mann" located along Kelly Drive. (It used to be called the East River Drive then.) I saw the Philadelphia group called the Soul Survivors.

I enjoyed Paul's performance a thousand times more!

How I got to see the musical icon was through the personal intervention of the Universe. I was late for a Buddhist retreat with the Tibetan Buddhist lama Lobsang Samten earlier in the day. Just as I opened the door at the Quaker building called the "Plymouth Meeting," I got a call on my cell-phone.

Leaving the building where some 10 people were chanting, I stepped outside and took the call. My good friend MaryCatherine was notified by one of her friends about the available tickets and she called me with the offer.

> Had I not been late, I would not have taken the call and my friend would have contacted someone else for the venue. The Divine Intelligence often does work in mysterious ways, both big and small!

What was stranger still was what happened to me earlier in the day. I had "tracked" the availability in Atlantic City for one of my all-time favorite Rock & Roll singers – Dion of "Dion and the Belmonts. I was asked to "track" three other artists and I couldn't find any I really liked but settled with Willie Nelson, the Rolling Stones and a group my son loves, a heavy metal one, called "Slipknot."

Less than an hour later I got invited to see one of my other all-time favorite artists through the benevolence of a kind and wonderful Universe. Thanks guys. Now I am truly *"Homeward Bound!"*

IV Vietnam War Stories

Grief delayed me while in military service

I WAS IN THE ARMY less than a week when the news hit me. Had my head shaven; my civilian clothes exchanged for fatigue pants and a shirt, not to mention boots and head-gear, something I had never worn before in my life.

Was drafted on the Third of June the day that Billie Jo McAllister jumped off the Tallahatchie Bridge. I was 19 years old, knew no one, and was away from my Philadelphia, PA, home for first time.

I quickly learned to fall into formation and step off with the left foot when hearing the command to march. I fell into step with the fellow in front, as well as those to the left and right of me.

I heard some guys talking, violating the sergeant's order not to speak while in formation and while marching. Had to pay attention to the pace being set by the cadence caller announcing in a loud, clear voice, to march "to you left . . . to your left . . . to your left, right, left," and then answering that same cadence crier who philosophized about loved ones we had just bidden goodbye:

> *"Ain't no use in going home;"*
> *Jody's got your girl and gone."*
> *"Sound off [One Two]; Sound off [Three, Four]."*

The noise around me continued. More marchers were talking. Louder! I couldn't grasp what was being said at first, but then I detected the word '*dead*' being used over and over again. Somebody had died. Somebody we all knew. This was June, 1968, at Ft. Bragg, NC, only a few days after being sworn in as a buck private. And then I experienced one of those moments like when you first heard the Twin Towers were struck, or of the assassination of a president decades earlier.

Bobby Kennedy is dead."

Couldn't grasp the words at first. Didn't want to. Here I was, a soldier, one who just swore to uphold the Constitution and do all in my power to protect the country. Couldn't vote. The leadership of the country then was something I never thought about. Learning the army's business was my only thought and goal.

"*Bobby Kennedy is dead*," the words came out again. Someone different this time. One with a Southern accent. The first had a Bronx accent or maybe one from New Orleans. They sounded alike to someone exposed to them for the first time. Mostly teenagers, hardly any of us near the age of 21.

"*Bobby Kennedy is dead*," this time, I was saying it to myself, as I stumbled and wanted desperately to stop playing soldier. I reverted to the just-out-of-high-school-graduate who learned of politics when the president -- LBJ --bailed out, and Bobby entered the presidential race. I liked him. He offered hope to people like me, just off the block, away from the village square, out from the farmland. For the first time.

"*Stop*," I wanted to shout. Stop the marching. Stop the life around me, the pounding, the moving, and the confining. Stop all of you. Let me be still. Let me pause in the moment. Reflect. Digest.

For God's sake, please let me grieve.

I needed time to take this in. Someone had shot and silenced perhaps the strongest voice against the Vietnam War and definitely, the most influential. Had he been elected, my life may have been different. No memories of fire-fights, lost comrades, death and destruction and . . . no PTSD (post-traumatic stress disorder).

Grief, however, eluded me. I was forced to put it off for another day, another place, another life. It was but a foreshadowing of more grief I would encounter before my career ended with the military. It's a grief I am only now dealing with through the practice of meditation and the Omega Institute Retreat on the *"Cost of War."*

But, that's another story. To be continued.

Going AWOL helps a boy grow into a man

WENT AWOL WHILE A PRIVATE in the US Army in 1968.

Had finished Basic Training at Ft. Bragg, North Carolina, and remained there an additional three long months, serving as a glorified *"gofer"* in a battalion commander's office, while awaiting a "secret clearance" to be completed. Had been away from home for no more than a few days prior to that. And when, at 19, I found myself transferred from the Deep South back North to New Jersey, I skipped out of Ft. Dix by going AWOL to my home in Philadelphia.

I didn't see it as *"Away without Official Leave."* I arrived on a Friday and did not have to report for Advanced Individual Training (AIT) until that Monday, and using my in-born initiative, I left the barracks and made my way to a bus station and then home.

My father had been mugged while I was away those past five months. Ended up in the hospital and probably caused his health to decline, forcing him to stop working at the age of 69. (Or was it 71 years old? You couldn't tell with Pop. *Achilles Contoveros* lied about his age. Federal records show two different dates of birth for him. One was probably offered by him under an alias when incarcerated for bootlegging in New York City.)

My family was in the process of moving from Brewerytown to Wayne, PA, a section of Philly's *"Main Line"* called Little Chicago. I liked their new digs and saw it briefly after finishing AIT and serving as an acting Corporal at a training camp later. But, I had but one stripe on my arm when I visited in late November.

I had sewed the stripe on myself. With needle and thread in a barracks where I lived without a radio, television or another soul for what seemed forever. Went cold turkey when I was drafted in June. Life as I knew it came to an end, as I got word of an outside world only by way of mouth. Didn't matter the first two months. A mean and nasty drill sergeant had given me no time for anything but army life, and he took pleasure on ordering additional push-ups for privates like me planning to attend Officer's Candidate School (OCS). That's why I needed the secret clearance. Couldn't have an enemy of the state upholding the Constitution while at war.

Going to OCS was my older brother's idea. *George Stanley Contos* was what we called a *"Lifer,"* one who'd spend at least 20 years in the military, thereby insuring a pension the rest of his life, plus PX privileges and other benefits. As a sergeant, he learned I scored well on leadership tests (don't know how; I barely made it through high school where I majored in *"lunch."*) He insisted I become an officer, believing military life would be better as a lieutenant than a non-commissioned officer. Ended up leading a combat infantry platoon in Vietnam. Got PTSD later. Thanks a lot, brother!

I got into a fight at 30th and Poplar streets in North Philadelphia during my visit home. You see, I wore my uniform and some street toughs wanted a piece of the *"soldier boy."* One of them threw something at me outside of *Merschen's Bar*, and I retaliated by grabbing a metal trash can lid and charged them gladiator style. We exchanged words, not blows, and went our separate ways with me upholding the reputation as one of our country's soon-to-be blossoming killing machines.

Returned to Ft. Dix and remember hearing the Beatles *"Hey Jude"* played over the radio for the first time. Wanted to cry. It was being introduced as an

"*Oldie,*" I thought, and I wanted to know where my life as a child had gone, how I found myself on the threshold of becoming a man. I missed my home, my friends, and my old girlfriend. I'd lose all of them over three years I'd serve in the Army. Be forced to grow up quicker on becoming an officer and leading boys only slightly younger than myself in combat less than two years later.

Got off with just a warning when the Company commander, a captain, called me into his office on my return. I explained my story in detail to him. He appreciated my candor, and declined to issue an Article 15, a non-judicial punishment, which would have prevented me from entering OCS. Learned there came a time when a person had to put away his childish ways and see the world as an adult. I did back then. But kept the memory of that child to let him loose now and then to tell a story or two. I gotta make sure, however, he doesn't go AWOL on me.

Abraham, Martin & John Live On Within

*R*AIN POURS ON ME OUTSIDE, *while soft music warms me on the inside. "Abraham, Martin and John," the song, plays from this relatively new gadget called a portable, hand-held, transistor radio.*

I'm on guard duty as a buck private, having been in the US army six months now. I'm wearing a slick poncho, an "OD" green-colored sheet of material that's like a rubber covering that got mixed with a device created just a decade earlier, called "plastic." The poncho is "yucky." Gives me the creeps. (I'll refuse to wear it again during my three-year military stint. Even in the rainy seasons in Vietnam and Panama. I'll let my clothes get soaking wet and allow them to dry, rather than permit the poncho snake-like feel on my bare skin.)

On this day in Ft. Dix, New Jersey, however, I wear a "steel-pot" helmet and carry an M-14 rifle beneath the poncho. Ducked into a makeshift tent when the rain fell hard. It kept pouring and there was nothing for me to do, but stare out into the torrential downpour and let my mind drift.

As well as turn on the radio. And hear Dion DiMucci, formerly with Dion & the Belmonts, sing a mournful song that was more Gospel-sounding than his usual teenage rock and roll efforts of "Teenager in Love" and "I Wonder Why," not to mention "The Wanderer" and "Runaround Sue."

He's singing of men who gave their lives for their country, their beliefs. Persons who placed their ideals above corporeal comfort. All shot down. All killed. And growing so much larger in the wake of their assassinations.

Didn't you love . . . the things that they stood for?
Didn't they try . . . to find some good . . . for you . . . and me?

It's taken me the entire length of the song, before realizing who Dion is actually singing about. John F. Kennedy and Martin Luther King come easy. But, I get stuck on Abraham. (And this morning, some 40 years later, I got stuck again when the phrase from that song came to me: ". . . is anybody wondering . . .?" Abraham arises in my mind. Abraham of the Bible, the Old Testament, and the father of our world's three major religions — Judaism, Muslim and Christianity. I began to "wonder" if the song is supposed to stretch back to that old man. The one with a long white beard who's prepared to kill his son — what was his name? Isaac? — and in performing such a sacrifice, pass a test imposed by the Lord.)

No way can I linger with this thought, and so I switch and focus on another relatively older, bearded man named Abraham. Abraham Lincoln, whose wife, Mary Todd Lincoln convinced her husband to host a spiritualist medium to conduct the first séance at the White House. It is that Abraham the song addresses.

Has anybody here seen my old friend Abraham?
Can you tell me where he's gone?
He freed a lot of people,
But it seems the good they die young.
You know, I just looked around and he's gone.

The song laments the death of two presidents and a great civil rights champion, and then poses a question that only came about because of tragedy occurring six months earlier to another Kennedy.

". . . Has anybody seen my old friend Bobby? I thought I saw him walk up over the hill, with Abraham, Martin and John."

The rain eventually stops. So does guard duty. But the song's message continues on through this day:

"*Find some good for you and me.*"

Pinned for a life above & beyond the call

WHILE NEIL ARMSTRONG WAS TAKING a giant leap for all mankind, I had taken a small step toward adulthood one month after the moon landing, and I had no one to thank for it except my brother, who encouraged me to aim for the stars in becoming an officer and a gentleman in the army of the United States of America.

I had weathered the worst six months of my life – worse even than my later combat duty in Vietnam – as I underwent the rigorous training in Officers' Candidate School. We ran everywhere we went, and when we couldn't run anymore, we'd run in place waiting in line for chow outside the mess hall, or to use the latrine. I was the second-youngest in a company of some 200 recruits – carrying a minimum rank of Specialist Five (E-5) – who learned tactics and survival skills and how to endure under the harshest conditions while developing leadership qualities. The youngest ones were targeted for even more physical and psychological drills because of our age.

The company commander once ordered me to do 400 sit-ups in a sleeping bag, relenting only after he got tired of counting, and I tore parts of my butt apart from sliding it back and forth against the ground so much. I'm surprised I didn't tear a hole through the bag, but instead of forcing me out of the program, it encouraged me not to quit and to take whatever he was willing to dish out. At age 20, with nothing but a high school diploma, I earned the respect of several with college and graduate degrees who might have changed their minds about my leading troops.

Those of us who made it filed out of the auditorium at Ft. Benning, Ga., having been addressed by some old weathered colonel who appeared to be in his 70s and was still jumping out of airplanes – his latest count reaching more than 600 jumps! He looked a little crazy, "gung-ho crazy," if you know what I mean. His eyes seemed permanently fixed wide open; he was jumpy and alert to the smallest sound or movement nearby. I would compare the hyper-awareness and sensitivity I'd get from post-traumatic stress years later to his demeanor and makeup.

But on this day, August 22, 1969, my oldest brother had prepared a ceremony to take place outside the doors of the graduation hall. Dressed in his regular working uniform as an E-6 (Staff Sergeant) he carefully removed two metal bars from a cardboard box. We called them "butter bars," the yellow metal bars symbolizing the rank of Second Lieutenant, the lowest rank in the Army's officer's corps.

So many things went through my mind as I stood at attention, looking straight ahead, hoping my dress-uniform hat was affixed properly. I didn't want to be out of order in any way, shape or form at this time in my life. What a moment!

My oldest brother, six years my senior, was about to pin the bars on my shoulder, officially welcoming me to a world where I would become an officer and a gentleman. I did not know then what the designation by an act of Congress would actually mean. That would come later in Vietnam, when I'd see mortar fire hit and wound half a squad I was leading; when a Viet Cong sniper would shoot and kill Lt. Vic Ellinger, one of only three lieutenants in our combat infantry company; or as two soldiers under another lieutenant's command would forget where they had placed their claymore mine trip-wire and walk into it, killing themselves.

That was all in the future, along with the PTS that would raise its ugly head some 25 years after the war. It wouldn't be all bad, particularly right after being discharged when this young veteran would use a sense of failure to achieve success in academics, getting degrees in journalism and history before finding his other life's calling years later as a public-defender trial lawyer after obtaining a Juris Doctor degree.

I knew none of this as my brother George fastened the metal bars to my uniform jacket, stepped back, and brought his right hand briskly to his forehead, saluting the superior officer that I had become. Nothing in my life could compare to that shining moment.

Wounds of Love Still Hurt this Soldier Boy

I took a deep breath and knocked on the door.

Peggy's mother, Mary, answered and said "*Hello Michael.*" She didn't invite me in, but smiled and I kind of smiled back.

I had dated Peggy for three years, starting at age 14. We had gone steady, but broke up a half dozen times, but I always thought we'd end up getting hitched someday. Particularly, after I was drafted and became an officer in the army.

And then I got that fateful message from my mother. I was in Ft. Polk, Louisiana, when I called from a pay phone back to Philadelphia and heard the devastating news.

"*Peggy got married,*" Mom said. I asked her what that meant and soon I learned Peggy McPeake married a fellow who operated a pizza store in the old neighborhood. He might have been an Armenian and not a Greek like me, I seem to recall.

I also recalled how I felt a stake was shoved through my chest. I couldn't breath and I felt I was going to pass out right there.

"How is she?" I asked Mary as she opened the door to her house, my heart in my hand. "Oh, the baby's fine," she said. "The baby's just fine."

"That's great" I said finally realizing she was talking about her grand-daughter. Not my Peggy. My Peggy no longer lived there. The Peggy I knew got married. That new Peggy was now a full-fledged mother and the wife of someone other than me.

I was never invited into the house where I had spent so much of my teenage years. I wanted to see the inside one more time, but I knew it would have been inappropriate for me to ask to come in.

It's over, Michael J. The romance is over and the door is about to close on it for good. Walk away with your pride intact, young man. Don't look back because she might see you crying. And a soldier in the United States of America on his way to war can't let anyone see how wounded lost love could make him feel.

Tibetan Book Winds its Way thru My Life

I GOT A CHILL WHEN I saw the word "Tibet" today because it took me back to the late 60s when I was a newly minted second lieutenant trying to make his way in the US army. The words that impressed me then, however, had nothing to do with the military. It had everything to do with life. Nearly 40 years later, I see that the "*Tibetan Book of the Dead*" called out to me, though I may not have known it then.

I had thirsted for more of an understanding of life back then. I was not quite 21 years of age. I purchased the book some two years earlier after learning of its importance by a source that might seem strange on the outside. Dr. Timothy Leery, the LSD guru who taught psychology at Harvard University and introduced the 1960s to the hippie phrase "*Turn on, Tune in & Drop out*" suggested the book for anyone wanting to seek a higher level of consciousness.

I read it from cover to cover while living in a rented trailer with another junior officer. I understood about one percent of the extraordinary dharma teaching about reincarnation and the Bardo, a place out of this world where your soul or consciousness resides for 49 days awaiting a new rebirth to help deal with the negative karma your past life could not get rid of. . .

Eventually, I put the book and all of its teachings aside, and raised no major questions as I got married, went to Vietnam and studied at the university before becoming a newspaper journalist.

At age 30, however, divorce was pending and my life once again begged me to seek a spiritual path. I met a young woman who led me to a guru, where I felt so comfortable visiting an ashram and listening to the talks in *"Satsang"* (*how did I just remember that term? I haven't thought of it for decades!*) I created a little "altar" with candles, incense and a picture of my guru, as I tried in vain to meditate, and on perhaps one occasion, I lost *"myself,"* and felt the most energized I have ever felt in my life.

(Spirituality called out to me again, describing in whispers of a state far higher than I had ever dreamed of before!)

But, life, my career and a second marriage led me away from that. I even dreamed of the guru leaving our Earth in a hot air balloon, drifting up to space, where I truly believed that he was going to perish while touching the outer atmosphere.

I awoke in a cold sweat, looked outside my tiny Pottstown, PA, apartment, and saw that it had snowed for the earliest time in eastern Pennsylvania's recorded history — Columbus Day, Oct. 12, 1980.

I grew a beard.
For the first time in my life.

I felt I had to rearrange something in my life, perhaps to ward me against some future threat, or prepare me for a new addition to my life style. Less than two months later, I met my future (and current wife, a so-called "Jesus freak") and she later confined to me that what drew her to me physically was MY BEARD!

Today, I have entered a new phase, where the *Tibetan Book of the Dead* is appending and writing a new chapter in my life. I will be going to a place called the "*Omega Institute*" for a retreat to contemplate PTSD (post-traumatic stress disorder), to meditate, and to study in a library, called the "*Ram Dass Library.*

Shades of Timothy Leary, LSD acid trips, and a book he and another brilliant young professor, Richard Alpert (a.k.a. Ram Dass), championed, "*The Tibetan Book of the Dead.*"

Am I coming full circle to something that started all those years ago and only now appears to come to a blossoming?

I would like to think so.

But why has it taken so long, and why did I have to squeeze through so many hoops, overcome so many obstacles, and avoid death and possible disgrace to finally get to "this" place?

I guess this is what one would call a rhetorical question? Maybe. But I still want to know.

Hoping for a lofty goal, I write a lot & often

I WAS A PRIVATE IN training as a soldier in Fort Dix, NJ, when I had a vision of what Buddhists call a "satori" – a moment of clarity about my life.

I needed to write a book.

Not just any book, but one where I was the hero. Well, hero may not be the right word. In the book, I was to be the center of attention while everything I'd write about would involve me and things that I had some sort of contact with. I used the model of the Bible as a guide.

I figured that the greatest book that there ever was should be the map and framework for my book. I'd be just like Christ, but not face crucifixion or circumcision. There was a driving force behind this idea. The idea stayed with me from the moment I was nineteen years old until I finished working for a living and found the leisure time to write about what I had discovered over the years.

I didn't know that I would write a book when I started dabbling with a blog. I started writing at **WordPress** the same month my Uncle Dom had died in 2009, and I guess I haven't stopped since then. The Blog became my way of expressing what I was seeing around me and what was happening to influence me. I learned that most of what I was learning was something I already knew, but had forgotten.

I think that much of spiritual knowledge is like that. We don't get our "smarts" from someone or some book out there. We get it from inside where true wisdom, love and hope resides. It takes some of us a lifetime, however, to realize that. All we needed to do was to become as silent as Dominick, smile, and hope to visit that wise child inside who has never left us. The child becomes the guide and offers us the inspiration to set goals and to eventually achieve them.

You're reading this right now, and that goes to show you that I achieved another step toward my goal. You can do it once you identify your goal and stick to it as if your life depended on it.

Your spiritual life will depend on it for you to follow through for your salvation.

Editor's note: Contoveros eventually wrote two books – "Francis of Assisi, a novel awakening to Lady Poverty" and "Ithaca Insights: A Mystical Odyssey." Both are available at Amazon.

Recalling some cool summers in the army

SUMMER ALWAYS SERVED AS A "new beginning" for me when I was in the army. I got drafted on the Third of June and did my basic training in the hot, dry air of Fort Bragg, North Carolina. I can't tell you how many push-ups I did during the two-month training session as the meanest drill sergeant I ever seen brought fire to my poor soul by running me everywhere and cussing me out to force me into fighting shape.

Worse was on the hot days when we were forced to carry heavy back packs as we marched through the hills and the leader would order us to "double time," that is, to run with such heavy burdens in the full sun. He'd watch sadistically, just waiting to prey on the first young man to fall out of formation and crash to the side of the path or the roadway. Those out of shape would be the first to hit the ground from either exhaustion or near heat-stroke. I remember how often I would pray just to hang in there to escape the sergeant's wrath.

I made it through basic training without falling out of line, but I was much less fortunate years later when I had to run three miles without a break. I had been out of shape after serving a year as a training officer in Fort Polk, Louisiana, where I continued to smoke cigarettes and drink on occasion.

I was in near perfect shape when I graduated from Officers Candidate School on August 22nd, that summer day just several weeks after Neil Armstrong had walked on the moon. I was awarded with the highest score in my company when scoring 492 in my PT "Physical Training" exercise, failing to reach a perfect 500-score after running a mile in six minutes and 12 seconds. (A 6-minute mile was a perfect score.)

But in order to get into "jump school" right before shipping out to Vietnam, I had to run three miles without taking a break. (You see, I wanted to toughen up before hitting the war zone and I volunteered to become a paratrooper and then join the ranks of the elite in becoming an Airborne Ranger.)

I couldn't stay up with the pack that humid summer day in Fort Benning, Georgia, and I got "recycled," that is, pushed back until I could attend the next three-week course.

Thankfully, I made it through the next run and jumped for joy in the process, getting "expelled" from a plane in four jumps and even parachuted out from a jet in one exercise. Unfortunately, I hit the ground running on my first jump and was nearly disqualified. You were taught to roll when striking the ground, thereby shifting the bulk of your weight away from your legs. I got hurt, but hid the pain from the observer who watched us land. I was lucky to hide the injury to my leg during the next four jumps and qualify for my wings, the pewter engraved medal worn only by paratroopers.

I never did become a Ranger. I like to think that the Universe conspired to keep me out of the rigorous program and to preserve my life while leading a group of regular "grunts" who made up my combat platoon. I'm happy to say that no one got killed while I was command those troops.

Summer hasn't been the same since I was discharged from the military and came back home from Vietnam on a hot July night. But I'll remember it every time my leg aches up and I get to tell war stories to family and friends.

11-Bravo & Combat Infantry Badge shine

THE PENNSYLVANIA LICENSE PLATE READ "11B-CIB" and it transformed me back some 40 years when I was in the army infantry running a platoon in Vietnam as a first lieutenant.

"11B" is what is called the "MOS" designation for a soldier and his trained skill. It stands for 11-Bravo or infantry.

The "CIB" stands for Combat Infantry Badge, perhaps the one medal servicemen of all ranks and persuasions have looked up to. It means that the bearer of this award or badge had faced enemy fire, or had been in combat.

Although I abhor war, I am still proud that as a young man was forced to engage in it. I didn't want to. I don't know of anyone from my generation that liked war, except some gung-ho types who ended up in West Point and often didn't know their ass from a hole in the ground. Or the one I served with who ratted out me and the company commander when we all snuck into Saigon one night and spent time with the ladies of the night.

We got caught and rather than go along with whatever the CO (commanding officer) offered as a lie, the West Point lieutenant could not tell a lie. He owned up to leaving the basecamp to see the harlots.

Well, the commander and I got no reprimands, but we never fully trusted that junior officer. He probably went on to become a general and got his rocks off in the first Gulf War under the first Bush presidency.

I kind of feel sorry for the guys who were never in the military. Not the ones that protested the war by escaping to Canada or signing on as a conscientious objector. They're heroes in my book. No, the ones I have compassion for are those that got a deferment because their father knew someone who could pull strings on their behalf.

They knew someone in government, or they could get a doctor to claim a sports injury was more than what it first appeared on paper or in an x-ray. It sure kept them out of harms' way.

But, I wonder what they did when the next life challenge occurred? When they got married and had to support a kid they weren't quite ready for, or discovered the marriage to the cheer-leader childhood sweetheart wasn't what it was all cracked up to be and she asked him for a divorce.

Challenges in life make one stronger. They also build character.

And while you couldn't ever pay enough to get me back into a war zone, I wouldn't give up my experience – or my badges of honor – for anything in the world.

Defense attorney regrets his prosecution

ALL OF MY LEGAL CAREER involved defending someone charged with crimes or offenses against the law. I worked 20 years as a lawyer, trying more than a hundred jury trials, winning more than half of them.

But to be honest, my first taste of arguing the law came not as a defense lawyer, but as a prosecutor, one appointed by some colonel to bring charges against a buck private who broke a law and faced a summary offense for some minor infraction.

I knew the young man. He was in the company in which I served as a training officer in Ft. Polk, LA. I even liked the kid.

I disliked having to "go after" him, but I took my oath to defend the US Constitution seriously. And I zealously presented the facts before a JAG lawyer (Judge Advocate General) serving as a judge.

I can't tell you how many times the judge — someone actually trained in the law as opposed to me, a second lieutenant with no college degree not to mention no law degree — admonished me for walking around the makeshift courtroom, pretending I was a Perry Mason cross-examining a witness. I was ordered to remain within three feet of a podium.

That restriction initially chilled my presentation, but I used my arms to wave and point into the air to get my thoughts across.

I secured a conviction. Something I fought against some twenty years later as a Philadelphia public defender.

But there was no celebration. And if I had to do it all over again, I wouldn't have taken the assignment but feigned an illness, if at all possible.

And, that's the truth, the whole truth and nothing but the truth, so help me God!

Can a Wrong ever serve as a Right?

"Conduct Unbecoming an Officer and a Gentleman" is what it's called.

NEVER THOUGHT AN AFFAIR I had with a married woman before turning 21 would qualify for *"conduct unbecoming,"* but looking back, I see how conflicted parties to such an act could easily become.

I didn't see it as morally wrong when I slept with an enlisted man's wife.

There. I placed it down on paper. And, I finally see how ugly it looks on the surface. How low and despicable one must have been to take part in such an affair. Just by reading it, one could easily believe I took advantage of a situation; that I used a higher position for my amusement, my gratification. And, never mind whose lives I could have destroyed and left in shambles.

Not sure how I met the red-haired German woman. She was a knock-out. All curves and smiles, and so much fun to laugh and drink with. The life of the party, who had an eye for me, a newly commissioned Second Lieutenant, assigned to a basic training company to help convert boys into men at Fort Polk, Louisiana. I cut a pretty good pose in my tailor-made uniform, if I do say so myself. Inexperienced in the ways of Love, but I was open to learning. And that's what pulled me toward this *"older woman"* whose husband left her stateside while he was ordered overseas. I never learned much about him or where he got stationed. Don't think I'd ever become involved with the woman if I believed he had been in Vietnam while I was with his spouse. And I didn't know she was married until I started falling for her.

Never saw it as adultery. Never thought of confessing it to get absolution for a sin, either. I was single. It wasn't like I was cheating on my wife or anything. She was. Cheating. (*Don't like using that word*) But, I never saw it that way. I saw a young woman who married an American soldier in haste, followed him to his home, and was unable to face alone the suffering a stranger in a strange land must endure to gain a certain comfort, a certain security.

I felt I provided her comfort and security. Helped ease the loneliness I knew she faced with no friends, no blood relatives, and in-laws who may or may not have accepted her or even extended a hand in trying to understand her.

She was vibrant, so full of life, so "*domineering*." She overwhelmed me at times. She helped pull me out of a shell. Had been reading the Tibetan Book of the Dead and contemplating a life above all "*pain and suffering*" when she swept into my Life, pushing all cerebral thoughts away, replacing them with down-to-earth, hearty earthly pleasures.

She taught me how to make love and care for someone you really loved. I made her feel at home again. Calm in the Eye of a Storm of Anxiety. I'd read to her. Yeah, she loved to hear me talk. Have been told I have a nice baritone voice. Sang back-up in an acapella Doo-Wop group, and can still hit a few good notes while in the shower or chanting at a Buddhist retreat. She loved the sound, and I'd often speak to her, while holding her as she closed her eyes in repose.

Was it true love we shared? I don't know. Forget how we parted, but it was amicable and no one learned of our secret. Our union made Life better for me, despite how illicit it was for us. I view her with such a kindness and loving fondness today. And I thank her for being there for me. I hope I was able to offer her with the same kind of memories. Sans any shame, or a feeling it was wrong.

Where is the boy I left at home for war?

I knew a boy
Who went to war,
And left his home
Behind him.
I knew him well,
That boy was me
And now I cannot
Find him.

A Vietnam veteran's tweak of a World War II sailor's song

Answers to questions about Vietnam War

1. *How did you feel when you realized you were drafted into the military?*

A 1. I actually "pushed up" my draft, after realizing I couldn't get out with a deferment due to a bad back. Had x-rays done, but to no avail. I was just what Uncle Sam was looking for, a 1-A Classification.

After notifying the Draft Board and getting one date to report, I asked the Board to delay my entry, so that I could go "in the draft" two weeks later along with one of my good friends from the neighborhood — someone I sang street-corner harmony with in Philly. We ended up doing basic training together, and met up more than a year and a half later in Ft. Polk, La., him as a sergeant, and me a lieutenant. He had just came back. I was about to go. To Vietnam.

2. *Did you support the war or were you against it?*

A 2. Did not care for war, but did not protest it. I did join Vietnam Veterans against the War while in college later, but took no active role. Just the membership fee to help end the war, no marches, no protests, etc.

3. *What did your friends and family say when you told them you had been drafted?*

A 3. My oldest brother was a "Lifer," one who made a career out of the military, and so my family was used to having a soldier in their midst. It helped him, and I know it helped to "straighten out" a lot of issues I had at age 19.

4. Were they supportive?

A 4. Mother and father did not have much to say when I went in. My brother guided me toward OCS, the officer's candidate school, Ft. Benning, Ga., after learning that I qualified. I guess someone saw some leadership qualities. I did say one of my heroes was Alexander the Great, and that I believed that one person really could make a difference in life.

5. What was the general reaction you received from people once you returned?

A 5. I wanted to avoid people when returning home. Robert DeNiro captured my feeling in the movie "*The Deerhunter*" when his character returned from Vietnam, and stood in the hills of a working class Pennsylvania town, looking down at the tavern where friends were planning his "welcome home" party, wanting no part of it. No one who has not been there — in the Vietnam War — could ever understand that we did not want, worst yet, believe we warranted, any type of a "hero's" welcoming. At least, I did not think of myself as "worthy." Don't know if it was due to the media, the general opposition to the war, or a sense of failure having battled so many of my own "demons" while in Southeastern Asia.

6. Were there any particular reactions that stood out to you? If so, what were they?

A 6. My second oldest brother, John, picked me up at the Philadelphia airport just a few days out of Vietnam, and he drove the speed limit on the area highway. I wanted to shoot him, but instead yelled and screamed, demanding that he "slow down" from the 55 miles per hour he was driving, not being used to such "reckless" speeds, and having survived by being cautious the previous year while living in Vietnam.

I enrolled in a community college. Attended a "sensitivity" session at the school before classes began. Sat on a floor in a circle with guys with hair down to their shoulders and young girls who loved how the long-haired guys looked and spoke. Talk about "cultural shock!" Thank God for a vets' club we founded on campus my first year back. It got me through it.

7. Do you think the government was supportive towards the Vietnam vets?

A 7. No. The military and the government did not understand the need for "closure" or "de-briefing." We needed time to adjust to a civilian world we had put behind us. We lived primarily with "survivor skills" that no longer fit in. We still retained the "flight or fight" instinct, and detested running away from something that scared us off. I "got myself up" to fight. A lot. Still do. Have only recently, in the past several years, learned to contemplate my next action when facing an anxious moment, but my first reaction has been just that — an "action," any action, and not freeze with indecision or immobility.

8. Do you think that the general population was supportive towards the vets?

A 8. People in the general population either feared the Vietnam veteran or forgot him. They did not want to dwell on something that most deemed a "failure," the Vietnam War. The biggest losers were us, the soldiers, marines, sailors and airmen that put on the uniform, only to face near ostracism on our return. Society refused to acknowledge the pain of losing — the colossal mistake our government made — and tried to deaden the pain we represented. It intentionally pushed the veteran off its radar screen. The fear and wariness was fanned by the Media. "Crazed Vietnam Veteran," was the headline inserted by newspaper copy editors when a reporter "dug up" a story with a vet committing a crime. Mostly all vets were seen as "killing machines," (Think Rambo!) even though only a few served in combat.

It got to the point where veterans left their military service off their resumes. It did more harm than good in getting a job.

9. Why do you think the Vietnam War was so unpopular?

A 9. There was an orchestrated effort by the most compassionate and highly intelligent segment of our society to end our nation's longest war. Done for the best intentions, it had disastrous results. The move to end the war was led by doctors, mental health experts, and liberal-thinking professionals who joined together to paint the war different from any in the history of the United States. Before the mental health agencies established something called "post-traumatic stress disorder" (PTSD and its predecessors, "Shell Shock" and "Battle Fatigue"), they came up with a separate and unique name for the rage, anger and lack of impulse control, entitled "The ***Post Vietnam Syndrome."*** They made this war out to be somehow "different" from all the other wars, that there was something so horribly atrocious about this conflict than any other. "Baby-killers" spewed from the mouths of only a few, but was heard by the ears of so many. Including those of us returning from war.

Lt. William Calley was convicted of doing no more than what a few of General Sherman officers condoned a little more than a hundred years earlier. "War is hell," is what we learned about Sherman's March through Georgia and the ugly underbelly of war.

"Hell is war" is the ugliness we had to learn from the Army's cover-up of cold-blooded murder. And the inability of a young officer to control his troops during a "skirmish" later called, the My Lai Massacre. He was the only one convicted of war crimes out of all who fired weapons on the 350-some women, children and a handful of elderly men in the small village area. The investigation showed many of the dead were sexually abused, beaten, tortured, and some of the bodies were found mutilated. The worst offense imaginable helped to turn most Americans against the war, but some politicians wanted a "Peace with Honor" and delayed the inevitable for years to follow.

10. Do you think that people during the 1960's had a realistic view of the war?

A 10. Americans knew only what our generals wanted them to know, and that came through the daily briefings in the safer rear areas where war correspondents were kept away from the real war events.

11. How did being in the war change your perceptions of it?

A 11. I never fought for God, mom's apple pie, or anything patriotic. Only fought for my men, the guy beside me, in front of me, and behind me. I fought even harder and wanted revenge when a "buddy" got hurt. But, I think I'd feel the same way if I was in a battle at home and not in a foreign land, whether or not I wore a uniform.

12. Did you participate in anti-war rallies once you returned? If so, did people ostracize you because you were a veteran?

A 12. Never took an active part against those still in the service. Joined and gave money for anti-war causes, but took no active role.

13. Do you think people's views of Vietnam veterans have changed in the past forty years? How so?

A 13. People have forgiven themselves and their veterans' for the mistakes our Country made. Wish we could admit to mistakes we are still making in the wars we wage today.

14. Do you think that the Iraq veterans can relate to the Vietnam veterans? Why?

A 14. Yes. We share the same confusion one faces in war when you don't know who might be the enemy. Sometimes, unfortunately, it can be a villager standing in front of you. A youngster (you learn later) who is playing with a booby trap, or drawing a soldier in to a spot where an explosive devise lay.

15. What words of advice would you give to Iraq veterans?

A 15. Keep the child-like innocence with you. The world ain't all-bad. Someday, you'll be able to enjoy the good in Life and be free of nightmares.

Most of the time that is. That won't come for a few years. Maybe. That's if you seek peace both within and outside of you Self.

*(Questions posed by **Emily S**., a sophomore at Creekview High School in Canton, Georgia, who is doing a project on the discrepancy between the treatment of Iraq and Vietnam Veterans. During her research, she said she "stumbled across" this blog. I had written about War while on Retreat at the Omega Institute "Hidden Cost of War" workshop. The words helped, she said. However, Emily had more questions. The above interview was conducted by e-mail today (April 28, 2010). And I am honored to have taken part.*

*Thank you, Emily. — Once upon a time, **Lt. Michael J Contos**, combat infantry platoon leader.*

War guilt haunts veteran year after year

I KNEW SOMETHING WAS WRONG when I saw the radio operator's face. He handed me the mike attached to the bulky radio strapped on his back. The private, new in-country, made no eye contact, and was hesitant in his actions.

I identified myself by a *"call sign"* and heard someone say in a code that the leader of the third platoon had just been shot and that I was ordered to move my first platoon to give him assistance.

First Lieutenant Victor Lee Ellinger had been fired on by a Viet Cong sniper. He was the best of the three platoon leaders in our Company C of some battalion of the 25th Division. (I can't remember the name of the battalion, which operated near Cu Chi. I block it. I hate the commander, even today. He's the only person I know whose own men tried to *"frag"* him with a hand grenade, but he escaped injury.)

Vic was a college-educated, good-looking "good old boy" with a thick head of blond hair and a Southern draw that got you to like him on first meeting. Had a large, bushy golden moustache, and a "swagger" about him that spelled out a *"natural-born leader."* Just like his namesake from his home-state, Virginia, Robert E. Lee. Vic hailed from Staunton, Va.

He was always on the ball and commanded respect form all his men, and wasn't afraid to *"raise hell"* like a drill sergeant when a slacker needed a little extra encouragement to do his duty, even if it only meant to "*police*" the area so the enemy could not find evidence of our movements, or worse yet, set a booby trap to a discarded C-ration can or an empty cardboard box that once held four loose cigarettes.

So, when I heard Vic was "*down*," I pushed myself harder than I ever did — force-marching my platoon to close the distance to get to him. Not sure how far we marched in the hot jungle creating our own path, with me walking point part of the way in my haste to help.

We got to his position. And, we were too late. Vic had died. Two of my men were medevacked out due to heat exhaustion they suffered during the march.

Never did find out the details of his death. We remained in the "*bush*" several days until returning to the "*rear*", where we attended a brief ceremony for Vic. My company commander said very little to the remaining two junior officers, even though we — I — had lost one of the closest friend we'd ever have in Vietnam. I never had the time to process Vic's death. I wanted to stop the war then and there. Wanted an answer to the question "*why*" he had to die? What were the circumstances? Why was the platoon leader shot and no one else? Was a sniper with the Viet Cong that good to take out the guy in charge with such skill?

I wanted to mourn him. To grief him. To set myself right by him. But I never did. Was ordered back to the "*field*" the next day.

Failing to grief him still haunts me. I have a sense of failure. And when I sink into deep depression, I wish it was me that got killed back then, rather than have to deal with PTSD (post-traumatic stress disorder).

You see, at times, I see Vic as the "*lucky one*," Me and the other platoon leader were relieved of our commands after "*friendly fire*" episodes. Two Second Platoon "*grunts*" who had set out a claymore mine for an ambush, forgot where they put the trip wire, and . . . walked into the wire, dying almost immediately. Their platoon leader was relieved. I got relieved when I had ordered mortar fire "*stepped down*" to get rounds to fall closer to the enemy, and the rounds fell on my own men injuring half a squad. I carry that guilt with me today. Good days and bad days. Meditation and bringing dark war wounds out to the light helps to ease the pain.

So does Omega Institute where I had written this while attending a retreat provided by Claude Anshin Thomas' called "*The Cost of War.*"

A taste of heaven offered here on earth

PIZZA PIE AND CHOCOLATE MILKSHAKE.

Each drew me like an oasis to a man walking alone in a desert.

But it was no sandy desert I remember traversing. It was the triple canopy jungle of Vietnam where the hot, humid heat would compete with any Sahara Sun blistering my throat, parched lips and dry mouth. And, I was not alone, but leading a platoon out of the *"bush"* where we survived another 14 days and looked forward to three days of *"rest"* in a rear encampment.

To hell with mom's apple pie and ice-cold lemonade. This city boy — raised in a melting pot called Philadelphia — wanted nothing less than ethnic foods made by ethnic hands.

Pizza with pepperoni! Hot with cheese that stuck to the piece as you tried to pull it apart, stretching the yellow substance as if it was a taffy. Further and further in the air as the strip of cheese would get slimmer and slimmer until it *"snapped"* and you made sure you got every little piece of it on top and not leave it in the tray for someone else to devour. You worked for that. You earned it. Remember how hot it was? Might have even burned your finger manipulating it with your hand and not a fork or a spoon. Who ate pizza with utensils anyway? You fought for that slither. You suffered a pain — no matter how slight — to get that extra mix of . . . what . . . mozzarella cheese?

And to place it in your mouth. That first bite. Almost heaven-like. Hell. **It was heaven.** Wasn't it? Particularly, if you closed your eyes and let the taste mingle with your tongue, your teeth munching away, your taste buds awakening to flavor of Italy, a touch of the old country, a hint of a big, loving abundant Italian mama.

And then a delicious milk shake made the old-fashioned way, not some McDonald's rip-off. The liquid mixture of milk, ice cream and whatever other ingredient the Jewish deli served up. Or one made by a young pharmacist's assistant at a drug store with a soda fountain. Like Mrs. Kaplan, the spouse of the local pharmacist, who'd create such "*joy*" in the Brewerytown section of Philadelphia (28th & Master Streets).

Nothing quite like the anticipation that for that drink. She'd use a long metal cup, fashioned for a special heavy-weight blender with three different speeds. No such thing as non-fat milk or ice cream when it came to a milk-shake. Pour in a little chocolate syrup and slowly churn it all together at low-speed. Hit a switch to get it moving quicker at medium, and then finally approach that high-speed where the whirling sound assured you that you're were about to be served a nectar a Greek god would offer a kiss from Aphrodite for. (Ok, a kiss from the god Ares for you young ladies!

Exposing myself and 25 other guys to fire-fights had nothing to do with halting the spread of Communism. Hell, I kinda liked the idea of a society where all are equal and share equally with our goods. (Like *Polish sausage, German salami, Swiss cheese, Lebanon bologna, Italian sausage* and *salami, English muffins, Greek olives, Danish pastry, French fries, and Canada Dry ginger ale* just to name a few of the internationally named products I'd fight for.)

(George Orwell's book, "Animal Farm," showed us some animals would become "*more equal*" than others. Particularly, when spirituality was removed from a country, the influencing goodness in humanity.)

So, I guess you could say that I fought for pizza and milkshakes. Rather, the right to enjoy 'em despite outsiders having no business being in places like Vietnam and Iraq. Not unless you're seeking a trading partner to introduce a new food or drink. Can we all say Chinese Egg Rolls? Japanese Saki?

It was me an enemy sniper was trying to kill

A Viet Cong sniper was trying to kill me. Some motherfucker hiding in the trees, the bushes, the triple-canopy jungle had just shot at my platoon. I thought he was shooting randomly, despite the debris from the ground, grassland and other tiny bits of rock that struck me from a bullet's ricochets.

No. he was aiming at no one but me! It's taken me more than forty years to figure that out.

Now I must try to answer the question, "Why I was spared?" and, what will I do now with my life after seeing I got a second chance to live it toward a more purposeful ending?

Christ Almighty! How could I not detect this assassination attempt on my life in 1970? We had heard all the stories about the life expectancy of lieutenants — especially the second lieutenants, the lowest of what are called "junior" officers.

"Sixteen minutes."

Yeah, you read that right. Some "urban legend," gave the new-in-country officer no more than the time it might take for a helicopter to touch down in a "Hot LZ," a landing zone where guns were blazing. Sixteen minutes was all the time it took for an enemy sharpshooter — a gifted sniper — to beam onto the newbie leaving the chopper to get his first salute in a combat zone. The lieutenant would end up dead before he'd finish returning that salute.

Who knows where that story originated? But there was some truth to it.

A sniper killed First Lieutenant Vic Ellinger, the leader of the Third Platoon, in my outfit, C Company. By all standards, he was a veteran, having been in the bush some three months before he was hit. The enemy killed no one else during the brief firefight. When he went down, the platoon sergeant called the company commander, who ordered me to help Vic's troops only to learn he had died while I force-marched my platoon. We had to medevac out two soldiers who suffered heat exhaustion during the long, hard, fast slug I put them through. A forced march is a journey in "quick time," a fast walk just slightly below a jog. Throw in a 20-pound backpack in sweltering heat over a distance of half a click (500 meters or half a kilometer) and it could be quite grueling to breathe, let alone march quickly.

I didn't bargain for this shit! Growing up in the city, I'd gotten into my share of fights, but no one ever shot at me.

But there I was, the man in charge. I never thought of the chaos a sniper could cause by shooting at the leader. He was out to get me and he had me in his sights. I did not know that then. (I thank God for temporary stupidity. It's kind of like temporary insanity, but that won't get you off in a court of law.) I never put the shooting together with the target of the shooter. I thought the sniper was simply pinning down the squad I was leading, not shooting directly at its leader, me.

I moved forward, but fell back when another round of fire rang out. Again, I felt some dirt and whatnot spray over me. But I still thought it was us as a group that he was shooting at.

The entire time I served in Vietnam, I never saw the enemy up close, and only got glimpses of him in a distance as we'd approach one of his encampments. I'd shoot in the direction of that glimpsed object, hoping I'd hit something or somebody. But I never knew whether it was me or someone else in my platoon who'd end up killing someone. We'd come across a body and that would be the only time I'd come face-to-face with "Charlie," the nickname we gave the enemy.

No one I knew in Vietnam ever engaged in hand-to-hand combat. We used no fixed bayonets, and I threw only two hand grenades the time I was in the field, because we hardly ever got close enough to heave 'em. We'd probably end up hitting a branch and have the explosion backfire had I tossed any more.

Had I known then that a real person was "gunning" for me, who knows if I would have acted any differently while at war? It would have shaken me, instilled more fear in me. I'd be more cautious and more tentative in my actions, following orders, and passing on orders.

Oh, I'd still go a little "berserk" when someone got shot, and revenge sparked a fury that made one's actions foolishly heroic. I'd charge like a madman when going to help a fallen soldier, as I did when learning that the third platoon had walked into an ambush and needed help from our platoon.

To hell with my safety; there were others worse off, and I believe I speak for every man I ever fought with by saying that any bravery we might have displayed arose from the love and compassion we had for the other guy.

What's keeping this vet alive all these years?

I survived the war in Vietnam. I was never wounded, although I developed a hearing loss from artillery fire and claim it as a disability with the Veterans Administration. There are lots of psychological scars that flare up when stress triggers a traumatic memory. It's called Post-Traumatic Stress (PTSD). But I am pretty much intact.

Today, however, I have a question that only a higher command can answer. Why was I spared? Why was another killed and not me? Is this just survivor guilt? I could have, perhaps I *should* have been shot. But why was I not?

More importantly, what have I done with a life that was given me by Fate or whatever power in the universe you want to name? What am I to do with *me* now?

'Cost of War' explodes at Omega Institute

I LOATHE MY INCONSISTENCIES ON grief, and how I dealt with death and injuries while serving in the military.

I blame the Army for not giving me the chance to mourn someone on first hearing of their senseless death. I blame myself for choosing to be a good soldier and not a compassionate human being, placing country first — before God and humanity.

I'd stuff all of my feelings deep inside and "carried on" with a "stiff upper lip" in face of the killings, when what I really needed, were a few quiet moments alone . . . to cry for loses to me and the many others such a tragedy produced.

"Bobby Kennedy is dead," went unanswered when I first heard the words a few hours into basic training at Ft. Bragg, NC. I was marching in formation, being "double-timed" away from the outside world, and into the new life of a soldier. A mean-looking drill sergeant with a "Smokey the Bear Hat" was "breaking us down" to "build us up" the army way. He was quite liberal in ordering us to hit the ground and "give me 20." Twenty push-ups, that is. "Give me 20" became his short-hand for any slacker he thought was not measuring up, and to drop to the prone position and begin the exercise.

"But sarge," I could have said," I need a silent moment to think about Bobby Kennedy."

Yeah, right. I was army property. Both body and mind, no matter what occurred outside the military compound.

And some 18 months later at the seasoned age of 21, I found myself with a similar need to grieve, but could not. I learned of the death of one of my buddies. I had only two, we three junior officers of a combat company in Vietnam became best friends, each leading an infantry platoon of mostly teenagers who, like me, were drafted, and unlike me, did not volunteer to be there.

The lieutenant was shot and I failed to get to him in time to aid him, not knowing whether a quicker response would have helped. It was one of those times that I wished I could stop the world from spinning, so that I could process not only his loss, but who I was as a man, and why I — all of us — are alive on this planet. At the least, I wanted a few moments to be alone, to grieve inside. Never got it then.

But the hypocrisy comes at the end of a tour of duty in Southeastern Asia, doesn't it Michael J? You had the chance to do something, but you chose not to. You and another young lieutenant were just days away from your DEROS date, the day when you were to leave Vietnam and return to the States. You served admirably and even got a 21-gun salute from the men of the mortar platoon you commanded near Chu Li with the 23rd Infantry Division. But you flunked the humanity test when you focused more on getting on the nearest helicopter out of the fire-base, rather than visit that fellow officer who lost an arm when chasing away Vietnamese children "playing" with trash outside the compound and an appendage got blown away while picking up an object with an explosive device attached to it. To this day, we Americans don't know if it was placed there by the children or not.

You had time to grief with him, to comfort him before he was taken to a hospital off-base. But you delayed. And he was flown away. You suppressed this memory until hearing a similar one at the PTSD retreat here in Omega Institute, called the "Cost of War." It came out through meditation practices.

Can't remember the fellow's name though. You blanked that out, just as you did the name of one of your best friends, Lt. Victor Lee Ellinger, until you traced him name on the "Wall" in Washington DC, several years ago.

Want no more parts of Vietnam, you told yourself when you were "Leaving on a Jet Plane." But you brought home with you a sense of failure, guilt and grieve, which you are finally learning to deal with now, without shame and without remorse.

Women Know the Help Boys Need in War

1917

The strange young man who comes to me
A soldier on a three day spree
He needs one night's cheap ecstasy
And a woman's arms to hide him
He greets me with a courtly bow
And hides his pain by acting proud
He drinks too much and he laughs too loud
How can I deny him?

Let us dance beneath the moon
I'll sing to you 'Claire de Lune'
The morning always comes too soon
But tonight the war is over
He speaks to me in schoolboy French
Of a soldier's life inside a trench
Of the look of death and the ghastly stench
I do my best to please him

He puts two roses in a vase
Two roses sadly out of place
Like the gallant smile on his haggard face
Playfully I tease him

Hold me 'neath the Paris skies
Let's not talk of how or why
Tomorrow's soon enough to die
But tonight the war is over
We make love too hard, too fast
He falls asleep, his face a mask
He wakes with the shakes, and he drinks from his flask
I put my arms around him

They die in the trenches and they die in the air
In Belgium and France the dead are everywhere
They die so, so fast there's no time to prepare
A decent grave to surround them
Old world glory, old world fame
The old world's gone, gone up in flames
Nothing will ever be the same
And nothing lasts forever
Oh, I'd pray for him but I've forgotten how
And there's nothing, nothing that can save him now
There's always another with the same funny bow
And who am I to deny them?

Lux aeterna Luceat eis
Domine, cum sancris tuis in aeternum
Quia pius es
Requiem aeternaum dona eis, Domine
Quia pius es
Requiem aeternaum dona eis, Domine
Quia pius es
Et lux perpetua luceat eis cum sancris tuis ina cap

1917

Through A Glass Darkly

(David Olney/Bug Music-David Olney Songs)

On Reading "1917"

I was never alone, was I?

Someone was with me. Someone knew enough about life. . And death to bring two bodies together. From the start of time, when a young man was called to defend something, something that some other felt important enough for another to die for. . .

She was there. *She* knew. *She* gave *herself.* No, she raised love to a level that was *divine.* Giving of one self so that another could escape war even for one night.

I can't stop the tears. I cry whole-heartedly now, letting my weakness show as I sob and wretch like a little old woman at the funeral of someone near and dear to her.

It started at the end. The end of this poem by some One who must have known what real war was about. The story evolved, the words took on a life of their own, and soon, the most beautiful young *Lady* I have ever known took control and comforted me, the soldier who displayed to all his courage, or at least put on that false mask day in and day out, unable to let it down for a second because other men depended on his stoicism. His strength. His hell that he faced at the front lines, inside the trenches, in the "bush."

How many poets, story-tellers, and Homer-like epic-writers does humanity need to see the futility of war, the destruction of pieces of young men, and young women?

Hard to stop myself. To get *"control"* of emotions I forgot I still had.

But I thank you for this. My men thank you for this understanding and the offer your *women* made for the boys in A Platoon, C Company.

Peace found inside middle of Vietnam War

I HAD LED MY PLATOON in Vietnam for several months when an unlikely event touched my life. We had encountered several fire-fights, but no one was killed or injured, thank God. But, you never knew what the next day would bring and so we were on edge, on the ready so to speak for anything that might have endangered us.

And then one day, I lead one of my two squads into an area where we came across a humongous crater that had been carved in the earth. I don't know what kind of bomb had created such a massive hole. It looked as if it had been done several years before the ten or twelve guys I was leading had approached it and circling it, decided to make our overnight "camp" there.

It was broad daylight, however, when we got to it and there was still several hours of light left. I'll tell you, I have never felt so much peace as I did when settling in at that moment. I don't know what it was that gave off such calm and relaxing vibrations. Perhaps there had been a monastery or some sort of temple there at one time. Perhaps spirits from those prayers offered up to whatever gods existed at their time were still lingering in the vicinity.

I felt secure and comfortable. I felt I could rest and not worry of any type of attack, even though we didn't let down our watch through the evening and overnight. It just seemed as if God had gathered us in his arms and was protecting us.

I hadn't felt that presence of God since I was twelve years old. I didn't recognize it as a "presence" until recently when I reflected on the more peaceful times in my life and determined that strangely enough, it was right smack in the middle of a war.

The peace came from within but also from the birds and critters that had returned to what must have been a burned out shell shortly after the massive explosion. Bushes and small trees had started to grow along the sides of the crater. There weren't that many flowers, but the foliage was pleasant to look at and comforting to believe it could conceal us from outside forces. Maybe it did.

And maybe that is what peace is all about, being able to go within protected from outside forces.

Well, it would be hard to imagine my peace in Vietnam being any better than what it was that day. It could have very easily been shattered by gunfire. Worse yet, the peace could have been destroyed with my heart and my soul wounded by something called friendly fire.

That's what happened during another incident while leading men on a search and destroy mission in what we called the "bush." I had called in mortar fire on a suspected enemy location, but one of the rounds fell on my squad. Five soldiers were injured and I thank God that none were killed.

But, being the man in charge, the lieutenant, I got blamed and I carried that shame and sense of utter failure with me all of my life. Peace evaded me throughout my adulthood as I battled what was labelled Post-Traumatic

Stress Disorder, an anxiety illness that causes flashbacks of the war when certain stressful situations trigger a physical, mental and emotional recall of the trauma.

I found peace, however, while attending a five-day meditation retreat, and I was able to journal about my war experience. I felt safe and secure among like-minded meditators. I figured I could cry like a baby while with them and they would still accept me despite my tears.

I did cry and it was refreshing. I also wrote about that day, the worst day of my life. And it brought peace to my heart. I saw how I had functioned as a calm and cool soldier under extreme conditions never losing my composure when chaos erupted all around me. I became detached from the scene, the carnage, and I did my job to the best of my ability and then some, if I do say so myself.

Inside, I felt myself shatter like a pane of glass struck by a wrecking ball aimed right at me.

It was the first time I was able to do this. Look at that dreadful day without recoiling and feeling the guilt, the anxiety, the grief and, worse yet, the shame. And I found that writing was indeed therapeutic. It is a method of meditation that I hope to continue over the rest of my life.

Peace is not found out there somewhere. It exists within, and can be found by focusing on that place inside that offers comfort, security and forgiveness.

Songs offered hope to Vietnam War grunts

MUSICAL REFRAINS FROM ROCK & Roll songs helped get me through the Vietnam War. I didn't know all the lyrics of the songs, only those short parts where I'd stop what I was doing and raise my voice in unison with the lead singer.

> *"We gotta get out of this place.*
> *If it's the last thing we ever do.*
> *We got to get out of this place.*
> *Girl, there's a better life for me and you!"*

I realized several years later that the song was expressing a young man's desire for him and his girlfriend to escape the community, the neighborhood that was keeping them from growing, from loving, and even from hoping.

Next came that wonderful sound we all sang in hopes of someday leaving Southeast Asia:

> *"I'm leaving . . .*
> *On a jet plane.*
> *Don't know when I'll be back again."*
> *Leaving on a jet plane.*
> *Leaving . . . "*

That was the offering from Peter, Paul and Mary, singing a song written by John Denver. Who cared what the rest of the words said or who it might have been addressed to? I felt I was leaving just about every time I heard the song. I needed to *"get out of this place"* when Eric Burdon and the Animals sang their music.

James Taylor provided us troops with several tunes, including "Fire and Rain." I listened to the music while resting with my platoon in the rear area of the jungle. The rear was a base camp, a secured area which saw minimal action, as opposed to the field or the "bush" where the grunts — the infantry men — would hump for fourteen days straight on search and destroy missions. You couldn't hear any music while humping in the bush, just the music of your heart beat reminding you to be careful where you walked.

The songs gave me hope. They reminded me of yesterday and the fabulous tomorrows that would come once your tour of duty would come to an end and all of us got back home safely.

(Fifty-five thousands of our young men from the United States and its territories' never made it back home.)

The only refrain I ever wanted to hear once I got out of Nam, was a folk song that sprung from an old Negro Spiritual. You'll never want to study war no more, my friend.

Down by the Riverside

I'm gonna lay down my sword and shield
Down by the riverside
Down by the riverside
Down by the riverside

I'm gonna lay down my sword and shield
Down by the riverside
I'm gonna study, study, war no more

I ain't gonna study war no more
Ain't gonna study war no more
I ain't gonna study war no more

I ain't gonna study war no more
Ain't gonna study war no more
I ain't gonna study war no more

I'm gonna lay down my heavy load
Down by the riverside
Down by the riverside
Down by the riverside

I'm gonna lay down my heavy load
Down by the riverside
Gonna study war no more

I ain't gonna study war no more
Ain't gonna study war no more
I ain't gonna study war no more
I ain't gonna study war no more
Ain't gonna study war no more
I ain't gonna study war no more

Finally, Light Shines on My Mutiny Quash

I LIED TO MY PLATOON to prevent a mutiny from bursting to a head some 40 years ago.

Today, I granted myself forgiveness. I cleansed a wound that never seemed to heal until now.

I served as a first lieutenant in Vietnam and was relieved of my command of an infantry platoon just two hours before getting orders to appear at a helicopter base port. Taken by surprise, I met the battalion commander who asked me to help avoid a military "disaster" from developing any further. My platoon of some 25 soldiers, grunts, as we liked being called, had refused to board the ships that would fly them into the "field" to patrol and engage the enemy. Most of the men sat on the heliport, reclining on their backpacks, disobeying all orders to climb aboard.

A day earlier, several members of the second squad were medevacked to a hospital after being ambushed by the Viet Cong. I had assigned a sergeant with some 10 years' experience to lead the squad. Unfortunately, he was "new in-country" and may not have had time to become acclimatized to the situation. In other words, he didn't know what to do in a war zone yet.

Our superior officer blamed me, the man in charge, and for the second time in my young military career, I found myself removed of my command. I was devastated the first time, and view that period as the lowest moment of my life. I felt lower than dirt and less useful than the ground below. At least dirt could be used to grow things and offer a structure to build on, I believed then.

This time, my being sacked hurt far less. I knew I had done everything to insure the wellbeing of my platoon, and instill in each member an esprit de corps that carried over into their individual lives. They learned to live for each other, to work as a unit, to place the needs of the platoon over their own.

It came as no shock when I heard they refused to go to the field! It was a mutiny, pure and simple. They protested what they believed was an outrageous act committed against them: the removal of their leader, Lieutenant Michael J Contos, yours truly.

(See Part II next)

My mutiny quash causes pride, sadness

I HAD NEVER FELT SO proud of anything — ever — as I was of their unselfish act of rebellion. For two hours, they put themselves on the line. No, they didn't expose themselves to a firefight. (That would come later). But, they were willing to face military sanctions, Article 15s and possibly a court-martial for someone they believed truly looked out for their welfare.

I ended up betraying their trust. I tried to convince them to end their holdout, to give up a fight they could not win. I could not agree with their arguments without showing a contempt and total disrespect for a superior officer, the battalion commander, who would be "passed over," not promoted because of a low "body count." He ended up relieving two out of the three young lieutenants in my company. The Viet Cong had shot and killed the third remaining junior officer.

I lied to this one young man I had "cross-trained" as a medic and a rifleman. He would fill in should we be unable to get to the regular medic, assigned to the squad. I remember speaking to him as if it was yesterday. He was from Brooklyn, New York. He reminded me of myself, a lot of spunk for a small guy, along with a bit of a "mouth" and very little respect for authority. "Tell me it isn't so," he said; that I wasn't "let go;" that I would continue to be their "LT."

Looking him in the eye. I told him what was needed to convince the others to get on the choppers and fly out of base camp. It was a lie. I lost a bit of innocence that day. I lost some integrity, a small part of my soul.

That has haunted me since. Until tonight, when I meditated with a group and we focused on healing past moments in our lives. By using this technique, I was able, for the first time, to view this incident *not* with the eyes of a 21-year-old inexperienced young man, but with the eyes of the *"Higher Self."* I knew what I did was right. As a matter of fact, I now know that I had the law to back me up. Criminal law, which I have learned from 20 years of practice.

You see, the common law, now codified into state statutes as well as in military practice, allows for a defense when a person commits one criminal act to prevent a far more serious act from occurring. For example, you break into a house to rescue someone from a fire. If you had not committed a burglary, the one in the house might have died.

Had I not taken the action I did, my men would have faced punishment under military law and the possibility of dishonorable discharges. I can now say I would have done the same thing, had I to do it all over again. Back then, however, I could not see that through the pain I felt. Nor did I have the wisdom to know the difference between one single principle and how an act of *love, compassion and understanding* could provide for the good of the many.

Comment

Nikolai Contoveros:

Very nice. You should tell me more of these stories!

Keeping all alive a lifetime achievement

AFTER SERVING IN THE VIETNAM War I turned my back on anything having to do with the military, and so I was totally surprised years later when requesting my medals, I got one that I still don't believe I earned.

How anti-war was I? Well, I joined Vietnam Veterans against the War, providing funds for a yearly membership. I wrote against the war in my college newspaper where I scribed as a reporter and then editor who eventually endorsed George Mc Govern for president of the United States against Richard Nixon and whatever secret plan he said he had to end the war. (My mom voted for Nixon four years earlier to keep me out of the draft and out of harm's way. The president didn't end the war, however, he escalated it!)

I stayed away from the Veterans' of Foreign Wars (VFW) and the American Legion because the members reminded me of old men who fought in "good' wars, particularly those veterans of World War II. They drank and reminisced about the glory of war, something that I found out ended with the first casualty on the battlefield. I saw no glory in fighting and only "got up for battle" when attacked and forced to come to the aid of a fellow soldier as adrenaline kicked in and I'd do anything to protect my men.

Looking back (and this gets a little painful; I don't recommend too many combat veterans do this outside of "group"), I realized that I fought in four major engagements when members of my platoon were injured. No one was ever killed. We never captured any enemy alive, although we obtained their munitions, food and supplies. I loathed the battalion commander who pushed for a higher "body count" and he remains one of only two persons I find difficult to forgive for his life's actions.

So when I opened the box with the medals sent to me by the army, it was surprising to see two that I was not aware of. I was proud of the combat infantry badge, the "CIB" that denotes that the wearer faced combat. I also liked the "wings" I earned for undergoing paratrooper training and jumping out of airplanes without breaking any legs.

But one of the "new" medals was given for flight into enemy territory. I earned a medal for the many times I climbed on the helicopter and took off flying into a landing zone not knowing who are what would greet us. You've seen those pictures from the war. Every time they're shown on television, I remember the young man who felt no fear jumping off a chopper and making his way to a secure area before determining whether it was clear for others to move on. (You couldn't pay me enough money to do it again.)

The real surprise was the other medal. For years I never knew what certain abbreviations on my discharge papers (DD-214) had stood for. I thought it was one of several medals everyone got for stepping foot into Vietnam, something like an individual service medal unique to the zone of Operation like the European Theatre or the Pacific Theater of World War II.

The letters were "BSA." It could have been for getting one of the highest grades on the rifle range while in basic training. I shot with precision, earning a sharpshooter or expert badge, which were two or three rankings higher than a "marksman." (I got the highest score in Physical Training (PT) during one extensive training session, missing a "perfect" rating by only 8 out of 500 points because I ran a mile in 6 minutes and 18 seconds, and not a flat 6 minutes.

Could "BSA" be the "best student award?"

No, it was the *Bronze Star Award*.

I don't know why I got it. But it has my name engraved on the back of a metal star apparently made of bronze hung below a colorful red and blue ribbon. I don't think I deserved it. My greatest accomplishment was to keep me and everyone who ever served with me alive.

Come to think of it, I'd gladly accept that kind of award anytime — to stay alive and flourish . . . in peacetime . . . or in war.

V Home from war and new career

Garrulous Greek' recalls journalism gift

I DISPLAY THE PEWTER PLAQUE prominently at my front door so that anyone leaving my house can see what has meant to me more than any awards I hang in my Feng Shui home.

The plaque was given to me by the editors and reporters of the college newspaper I served on as editor-in-chief. It was called "The Communitarian" and provided news for students and faculty at the Delaware County Community College just outside of Philadelphia

I became the chief by default. A young woman much smarter and a much better writer – Alice Brown – couldn't finish the job because she was a single mom raising a small boy and didn't have the time for extracurricular activities. Me, I could barely write a sentence without having spelling or grammar errors. But I had fortitude or maybe something called gumption.

You see, I had just finished my first year as a student after serving in the Vietnam War and I wanted to prove that veterans were not losers or crazed men. I pushed the reporters to write more and turned a quarterly newspaper into a weekly one with special editions on the 1972 election and my favorite, an April fool's edition. I was in charge, and with the consent of the staff, I endorsed George McGovern, risking the ire of many of the faculty who supported the eventual president, Richard Nixon.

The April Fools edition showed a greyhound dog lifting one of its legs in an attempt to relieve itself on the masthead of the newspaper. The person that applied the photo of the dog said that he actually "cringed" while using an X-Acto knife to cut sharply below the dog's private parts. (Ouch!) Inside, we ran a quarter page advertisement offending a lot of the student feminists by asking "Pregnant? Need Help? Call us for to get you with child!"

I enjoyed meeting deadlines. It reminded me of firefights and the thrill of facing the uncertainty of the moment. I became a trial lawyer years later and loved trying a case from the proverbial "seat of my pants." I guess I got hooked on risk-taking and sought it out most of my life.

The plaque gifted me at a special dinner of fellow students and our faculty advisor was the best award I ever got — that year or any other year. I had also been awarded a Sigma Delta Chi journalism scholarship and a James A Finnegan fellowship to study state government in Harrisburg because of my editorial strivings. In addition, I was also chosen as a student speaker to address the graduation class where I angered many of Republican school district leaders when I pointed out the faults of a president facing obstruction of justice violations for something called "Watergate."

It is this plaque, however, that has helped me get through some tough times when I felt really down. It's made out to me *"the Garrulous Greek"* for *"the horizons we all reached"* in journalism and in life.

I'll never forget how touched I was then and how it is still warms my heart these many years later!

Graduation highlights father-son ties

One of the most wonderful moments of my life occurred without my knowledge of it. Had I the presence of mind to be more present for things that mattered, I might not have missed it. Recalling what this once-in-a-lifetime occurrence must have been like, however, is the second-best way I know of memorializing it.

IT HAPPENED WHEN I HAD got a graduate degree at Temple University in Philadelphia during the Bicentennial Year, 1976. The country was 200 years old, and I had studied colonial history, hoping to turn the knowledge into a salable commodity — that is, writing history for a newspaper.

I chose history because, first, I always liked it, having been "turned on" in grade school when a nun told us of the glory of Greece, the land my father had come from in the early 20th Century. The second reason was that history was one of the few graduate courses that did not require two years of language. I might have majored in English had it not been for that requirement.

How I ever got this far in higher education, I'll never know. I barely made it through high school, graduating from a vocational-technical school where I learned to be a printer. I made it despite having been suspended from the trade school, Dobbins, and earlier, the Catholic school, Bishop Neumann, where I had transferred out after playing hooky.

I cut so many classes my senior year that when I look back, I can't understand how I got the requisite state days for class attendance. I'd come to school late, sign in at admissions, and someone would mark me "present," but late. I'd skip the classes I didn't like, and never get caught, because each teacher would see my name on the attendance sheet as "absent." I ended up with nearly perfect attendance, but boy, what a record I got for tardiness!

Forget about college on graduation. I never would have made it at age 17. I had too many social plans to keep, girls to meet, and a job to seek. Who cared about cracking the books when you had the whole wide world outside your home to study?

It wasn't until Uncle Sam drafted me, and I spent three years away from home — one of those years in Vietnam — that I saw the true value of an education. I'd looked at all lackluster officers in the Army, and said to myself, "If those dummies could go to college, I could, too."

I became the first in my family to enter the halls of ivy, first attending Delaware Community College (my favorite school), then transferring with enough credits to get a B.A. from Temple in one calendar year that consisted of three semesters

Still having credit under the GI Bill, I decided to seek a graduate degree. (Not being able to find a job had a lot to do with that.) So I used up the full 48 months of stipend from the government, and reflected on my life when the college asked students to submit something in writing that they thought unusual or out of the ordinary for graduation. I finished my classes August 1975, but would not graduate until May 1976.

By then, two part-time jobs occupied most of my time, so I made no plans to attend graduation or let my family see me among the pomp and circumstance. I had spoken at commencement at the community college two years earlier, and had skipped graduation for a B.A. in journalism. I thought nothing could top the feeling I got attacking Richard Nixon and Watergate in my unedited talk to students and the mostly Republican college trustees of suburban Philadelphia.

It wasn't until two close friends who attended the 1976 graduation visited me and my father and told us what we had missed. Marvin Wachman, then president of the college, addressed hundreds of graduates.

He told them the story of my father, Achilles Contoveros, who never made it beyond sixth grade at his home on the tiny island of Nysiros, Greece, but attended that day to watch his son get a master's degree in American History.

I got chills when they told me this. I had never expected it. Neither did my pop. I knew it meant the world to him, because his last words before dying two years later were "God Bless America," in the thick Greek accent he never was able to graduate above.

We did it for you, Dad.

Willie, 20 years later, I still mourn you

Although you "passed on" after your 17th birthday, you'll remain alive for me forever. I see you in my dreams. I "feel" your presence as I walk with you, watch you, and hear the footsteps on the steps leading from the dining room to the bedroom upstairs.

YOU APPEAR IN THE SUB-CONSCIOUS, along with my brother, George and my parents, who often show up in a dream. And of course, there's my other best friend, Johnny Keller, who says little but knows so much in this *"after life"* that appears while I sleep. And where those who died, live on.

I still see your *"hang-dog"* look when you were young and ate up half the brownies left out to cool. You got sick, but knew as soon as you saw me, that you did a *"bad"* thing. *"Woofing down"* such rich chocolate delights and being unwilling to share with others, had I not caught you in the act.

And the same with the pizza I left out. I should have shut the lid, but I was just going into another room, only to return discovering most of the cheese and half the pepperoni missing from the top of the pizza pie. Never did learn where you had snuck off to *"lick your chops"* after scoring such a delicacy.

Willie. Can't say the name without getting a little choked up. You have become the symbol in my Life for all that represents loving kindness and compassion. Even though, I was never the only one you brought joy to, I felt singled out, devoted to by you. Remember when PaPa came to visit and spend the night alone with you? You left your bed, climbed onto his, and — not content with simply lying beside him — you "*nosed*" your way beneath the covers and gave him one of those "*puppy dog*" looks you were so good at projecting to others. All others.

Got a portrait that memorialized you. It's framed and hanging for all to see. The best one, however, is the one that only I can see. The one of you in my dreams.

Willie. My best friend.

Willie. My perpetual guide in the "*Other World.*"

Willie my dog.

Newspapering requires typing correct obit

"The quick brown fox jumped over the lazy dog."

I TYPED THIS OVER AND over again, hoping that I'd learn the fine skill of typing as I sat in a class with all girls. Young women, I should say. I was the only male in the Delaware County Community College course of study and I never once felt out of place or unusual.

I wanted to be a journalist, you see. So, I figured I had to learn the fine art of typing in order to file my stories.

"The quick brown fox jumped over the lazy dog" was one of the lines I'd type to get proficient at the skill. Another was *"Now is the time for all good men to come to the aid of their party."* I don't know how many keys I touched typing that one. I didn't even know what party the keyboard operator might have been talking about.

But I quickly learned how to type and it came in handy some three years later when I finally got a job as a newspaper reporter in Pottstown, a small working class town some 30 miles outside of Philadelphia.

I remember having fun whenever I had to take an obituary. Yeah, an obit. From a funeral director. The city desk at the Pottstown Mercury Newspaper would direct the calls from outside to whatever reporter was not busy and as a new recruit, I got my fill of 'em.

I'll never live down the first one I did involving a Catholic funeral. I got everything right about the guy's name, his job and his relatives. But I blew it when I wrote about the church services.

"A 'massive' Christian Burial will be offered at St. Pius X Church," I wrote and turned in the copy.

I heard laughter from one of the copy editors. Soon, other editors had joined in laughing and then I realized they were laughing at my obituary.

The obit should have said "A 'Mass of' Christian burial would be held" . . . instead of the word "massive."

Typing ain't bad as long as you got a good editor to catch what I call your "lazy ear" mistakes.

Reporting the news takes courage & trust

MOST OF WHAT I LEARNED about journalism came from observing a true crime reporter named *Michael Sangiacomo*.

I was just hired by the *Pottstown Mercury*, a small newspaper some 25 miles outside of Philadelphia (and the home of *Mrs. Smith's Pies*), when Sang (Pronounced Sange, as in *"Angie"*) took me under his wing and showed me the ropes.

Never, never reveal your source, he said. And always attribute your source whenever you can.

Sound like gibberish? A contradiction in terms? Let me explain. A source of information would dry up if he or she thought their name, provided you *"off the record,"* would appear in print. Or if they fed you news strictly for *"background information."* One is self-explanatory, while the other, for *"background"* purposes, permits a reporter to provide information unattributed yet reliable, because a reporter's well-known source is providing a necessary context to understand something. Usually, something controversial, borderline illegal, or both. A good reporter would go to jail before giving up such a source.

Revealing a name could lead to a firing or worse, depending on any strong-armed connections. (I got driven off the road once when uncovering inside information about a homicide outside Phoenixville, PA. Never had anyone pull a gun on me, but almost got run over after writing one story. And that involved a minister of a church being defrocked!)

Most people enjoy seeing their names in the paper, particularly, if they're in authority and you get your facts right in the first place. That's straight from the Sangiacomo playbook. Feature stories always cheered up people, he'd add. The more names you could drop, the more readers there'd be. The more people who would clip out a newspaper story and put it on a bulletin board or in a scrap book for long-term viewing.

That would include tragedies. Simply to show history of sorts in the making, like a fire to a favorite store, or the closing of movie theater falling prey to the multi-screen complexes at a new mall.

Some cops would be offended if you didn't mention their name making an arrest. That included at least one detective, of whom, incidentally, Sang and I both considered not the best on the force. The quiet, reserved publicity-shy investigator always turned out to know more than anyone else but didn't need everyone — including the public — to know that he knew it.

Sang knew how to groom a source. He'd put himself out to gain trust, something law enforcement folk find rare in the Press, and when they did, they'd treasure it. Sangiacomo would get calls the major papers would not, and be privy to the inside dope when a national news story would come our way.

Like a hostage-taking incident at *Graterford State Prison*, near Collegeville, Montgomery County, when a few correctional officers were overtaken and held by inmates one day. News agencies feeding information world-wide could not compete with Sangiacomo's reporting. His name and that of our 30,000 circulation newspaper would be quoted frequently even though no one ever copyrighted any story. The attribution was done as a professional courtesy to a trusted colleague.

And, Sang would be generous with others. I got several state awards for reporting *"piggy-back"* on some of his stories, following up on articles that demanded attention day after day, like that of a murder mystery of a local businessman, which was leaked to us, the newspaper reporters, to help in the investigation.

The stories would never have seen the light of day, if it were not for the trust and belief one had in a fellow like Sangiacomo. Thanks, my good buddy. Copy you again sometime at your other newspaper, the Cleveland Plain Dealer in Ohio.

Truth once hidden usually surfaces later

"State Trooper Using Hypnosis for INESTIGATION" read the headline for one of the strangest cases I ever reported.

While working the *"late shift"* at the Pottstown Mercury, I heard the highly excited voices of the police dispatcher over a radio scanner describing a shooting and the words *"officer down."* It was moments before deadline for the newspaper, and I quickly called the Embreeville State Trooper Barracks in Chester County, Pennsylvania. The city editor pushed back the deadline and remade the front page, as I somehow gathered facts for an incredible story.

While stopping a possible stolen car, a Pennsylvania state trooper fired his gun before being knocked unconscious by the driver who got away. He recovered after being treated and released, but was only able to remember part of the license plate number, and our paper with its 30,000-circulation printed a request for anyone with information matching a description of the car and the driver be provided the police.

It was exciting being a police reporter. You were on top of crimes — often as they were taking place. One of our staff members won a Pulitzer Prize for "Spot News" photography when he responded to a similar "call" over a police scanner, drove to the crime scene, and took pictures of a crazed bearded man with blood streaked across a bare chest and bare-footed rushing toward a cop with a knife in hand. Tom Kelly snapped the picture seconds before police arrested the man — Richard Greist — for killing his wife and cutting the fetus growing inside of her while attacking other family members. It took courage to snap the picture, placing his art, his craft and his job above his own safety. Kelly's the type of person I'd want with me while life from a foxhole.

Many journalists would place the "story" above their own welfare, digging for details when they smelled corruption, and walking the extra mile for the downtrodden victim of some tragedy, perhaps a fire or flood. My state trooper story grew into a little of both.

> *You see, I traced the state trooper to his home. By luck, I scanned the Yellow Pages and called the number of the fellow with the same name as the injured trooper. Voila! It was him! And, I got one of the greatest stories of the year.*

The trooper had agreed to undergo extensive hypnosis to try to help recall details of the incident. He shared the details with me, as I took notes on something called a "*typewriter*." We did not transition to computers until the late 1970s, and I gathered facts the old fashioned way. By the stroke of a key noisily striking "*copy*" paper placed in an old Remington Typewriter.

What a fascinating story. I released it to the Associated Press and it went out internationally. How often do police resort to such tactics as part of an investigation, let alone reveal this to a public only awakening then to the hidden powers of the unconscious mind?

The story had "*legs*," as we'd say in the business. Wrote four or five follow-up stories and was contacted by magazine and television reporters trying to get information about my source, with me declining to give up the name or number of my goose that was laying the golden egg.

The story died out, as most do. There was no mention of the incident until several months later. I'm glad that my newspaper gave the new twist the same coverage — the top story of the day. But, the tone was much more somber.

The state trooper was released from the police force. He was ordered to undergo psychological treatment as part of an agreement for no charges to be pressed against him for lying. The young man, new to the life as a law-enforcer, accidentally fired his gun. And rather than own up to such a mishap, he created this story to appease supervisors who demanded written reports when a weapon was discharged. It was a Big Lie, one that got bigger with his willingness to be hypnotized. A lie I helped to perpetuate each time I gave it play through my police reporting.

I learned the truth could be manipulated at times, but that staying true to it was always the best policy in the long run. I hope the state trooper, no matter where he is today, had learned that same lesson.

Three Mile Island 'melts down' with memories

THE LOOMING TOWERS OF THREE Mile Island (TMI) grew in size as I drove from Conshohocken to Harrisburg, PA, some 90 miles away. It was on this very day, March 29, 31 years ago, that America experienced fear and a second-guessing of its decision to build nuclear reactors so close to populated areas.

I entered the grounds as one of only six reporters to tell the world what it was like inside a facility that had just weathered a partial melt-down, far worse than what had been described in the movie with Jane Fonda and a young Michael Douglass, the *"China Syndrome."* The movie's title came from scientists' theories that such a meltdown of a nuclear core could burn all the way to China from a place like . . . would you believe the movie, filmed before the accident, actually referred to the state of *"Pennsylvania."* What a coincidence. Or was it synchronicity?

President Jimmy Carter had *"toured"* the plant a few days earlier. Himself an engineer, he wanted to insure to Americans that there was no fear of the plant. It helped. So did the cool-headedness of then Pennsylvania Gov. Richard Thornburgh, who later served as US Attorney General.

I compared Three-Mile Island to the plant being built in Limerick, PA, some 25 miles outside of Philadelphia. Nothing I wrote as a *"pool reporter"* is memorable today. I described routine activities like employees working at the job site, a man's ability to forge on despite accidents, and the cleanliness of the facility — except for some graffiti that our Pulitzer-prize winning photographer captured for the story.

But, it had very little criticism and probably got very little exposure in a period when "*bad news*" travelled a helluva lot faster than the good stuff.

Today, TMI is just a "*blimp*" in America's history. But anyone who lived close to it back then, can tell you of the evacuation of nearby towns and the record volume of telephone calls made to Pennsylvania from loved ones out-of-state. If someone even remotely connected to the area told you they weren't scared, don't believe them. We all were. Some won't admit it.

One thing about my TMI story stood out, however. It was actually a follow-up I wrote weeks later. I got a letter from Metropolitan Edison Co. (Met Ed), the operators of the power plant. (They went out of business or merged into some other utility conglomerate, I believe. Used to have "*Snoopy*" of the now defunct "*Peanuts*" cartoon strip as its advertising mascot. Have no idea what Charles M. Schulz, the artist of Peanuts, ever thought of his creation and its commercial use after March 28, 1979.)

Each reporter was given a plastic pin that we carried on our chests. It was to measure any exposure to radiation. At the end of the day, you turned in the pin and weeks later you got notification from the company.

Got no radiation exposure, according to the letter from MetEd. Kept that letter and actually framed it. You see, the company that was trying to show the world that there would never be any other mistakes in managing the use of nuclear energy had proven to me how fallible they truly were.

They made a mistake with my zip code. Got it completely wrong. Did not even come close and actually printed out a code for someplace out west, I seem to recall. Human error? Or machine? Did it really matter back then?

How about today?

Going back home sans the Maidenform bra

WHAT'S THE BIGGEST LIE YOU ever told?

I'm talking "*whopper*" now. None of the "*little white lies*" kinda story. But one that would qualify as a bold-faced LIE!

Mine was to an ex-girlfriend. Not a lie to hide I had been with another girl. Or why I forgot an anniversary or her birthday.

I told Peggy McPeake I was a homosexual so that I would not have to go to bed with her. It was a lie. And I'm not. Not that here's anything wrong with it. But, I couldn't think of any other reason not to hurt her feelings.

Oh, I wanted to "*be with her.*" She was one hot number. And I was turned on to her when I saw her more than 10 years after we had broken up, married others, and eventually divorced. We were both divorce-free, ready and able to consummate what we had wanted to do during the three to four years we dated, but refrained from doing.

It just didn't feel right.

Before anyone starts to call me a "*wuss,*" and claim I should have pulled a "*wham, bam, thank you 'mam,*" let me explain. It wasn't the same at age 30 as it was at 14 through 17. She wasn't someone I could treat as a "*one-night*" stand, walk away from, and forget about.

She was the girl I "*knew*" I would marry one day. So sure of myself when I was a teenager. Everything was black and white, good or bad, them versus us. It took years to learn that opposite's sides of a coin always merge at the edges. That many, if not most, of life's decisions are made from a gray area.

Peggy had two children. Both had been put to bed by the time I visited her at her house in the old neighborhood of Brewerytown, North Philadelphia. She had straightened up, but someone had poured leftover Cheerios into sink-full of dishwater, and I could not shake the image of little round oats floating around when we "*made out*" on the couch.

Nor could I get use to the metal I felt around her bra. Had never "*felt*" one of those "*up lifters*" before that night, and thought perhaps it was a prosthetic device for some broken parts. It got in the way of truly "*feeling*" her, the way I remembered her.

Couldn't get the thought of her kids sleeping nearby and possibly walking in on us. I wasn't ready for another marriage at that moment, and that's where this may have gone, should we have taken that next step. You combine all of this, plus the nagging belief we were not the same persons we were in the '60s, not the same teenage couple, not of the same chemistry as before.

And that's when I decided to lie. Not only to let her down easily, but to "*let myself up*" from possibly making the mistake some believe they will never make. That you can go back home again. To become the same persons you were again.

Too many things change. They mold us for better or worse, and while it would be so comforting to renew an old loving way of life, Destiny and Fate most always demand we seek our futures elsewhere.

And that's the truth, Peg. Can you understand it now?

I'm heartily sorry for having offended thee

"Michael J,

THE BIGGEST LIE YOU EVER told was that you could say something about sexual orientation and not hurt someone whose way of life might be different from yours. You said you lied when you told an ex-girlfriend that you were gay to avoid having sex with someone you were not ready to have a long-term commitment.

You treated homosexuality as if it was a bad thing. Probably because of the way you were raised, and the fights you got in to prove how "*macho*" you were and that there were no feminine traits in your make-up.

Ha! We are male and female alike, you dummy. Some of the things you love in life are considered by Western standards as *feminine*. Love itself, the *longing and the yearning* to be with a Love is not deemed as a strength, a *he-man* quality, but the soft, gentle caring from your better side, yes, the feminine side.

No, you're not gay. And you can say "*not that there's anything wrong with it*," and believe you covered yourself. That you haven't hurt anyone's feelings. But, what if you were? What if you lived life outside as a woman, but inside as a man? Or the opposite?

What would be your biggest lie? That you did not have feelings for someone of the same-sex? Your whole life would be a lie, feeling you had to please your parents and date at a certain age, or find the right "*girl*" to go with you to the prom.

Or even marry because you remained confused and unaccepting of who your really are due mostly to what your small society, the community in which you were raised, dictated you follow such a path, such a way of life?

What would Buddha do if he found himself in this predicament? Well, he never would have written about Peggy McPeake in the first place. And you know he would have been straight with her and simply told her he enjoyed her company, but was too hurt from a broken marriage to think of entering another one so soon with a person he loved as a child, but really did not know some 10 to 12 years later. A young woman who didn't know the type of man you had become. Or failed to become.

What if the Buddha had done the above before he was enlightened? Before taking his vows? Before realizing the Middle Path was the best path to stay in the state of Nirvana?

Perhaps, he would have said that his intent was good, but he lacked the true wisdom to see how his speech was not right, but wrong. That it harmed someone, that hurting even one person was one person too many to cause a suffering in a world you hope to ease the suffering for everyone.

Ask for forgiveness, strive for good merits and try to walk in the light more, Michael. That's the best way to seek enlightenment.

Bow, move on, and try to keep your head out of your butt next time."

(Mea Culpa provided for: *Going back home*)

You man a job right, job will right the man

⤙

JOBS HAVE A WAY OF defining us. We become "*the job*" or rather grow into what we perceive to be the "*ideal performer*" of that job. Whether we like it or. The job. Or ourselves.

I loved civil service jobs. They were among the best I had. Worked for the Pennsylvania Department of Transportation (PennDOT) as a "*information specialist,*" and served as an intern for the Defender Association of Philadelphia representing poor criminal defendants. Both were summer jobs!

The first involved writing as a Finnegan Fellowship student between my 2nd and 3rd/4th years in college. (Combined the two. Earned enough credits to graduate in three, and not four years.) Answered letters and fielded phone calls in Harrisburg, the state capital of Pennsylvania, as part of a fellowship to study government while working in the "*field*." Ended up writing press releases, a speech for then Gov. Milton Shapp, and doing the "*voice over*" for a television newscast at a local TV station. I got the job despite limited writing abilities. Studied journalism right out of the Army, never thinking writing could become a "*career*" until a neighbor asked me on entering Community College what I was to major in. I didn't know. He suggested Journalism because I studied printing. He thought they were closely related.

Well, yes and no. The graphics part is related, that is, the "*make up*" of the printed word is a form of communications. You can attract interest in words by the way they're presented. But printing does not involve "*writing*" the editorial content, the thought process to convey ideas. I had no background whatsoever in writing while in high school year, or three years I served in the US Army. I wrote a smidgen of poetry and one short story looking at my family's move from Philadelphia to the suburban Main Line Wayne, PA. (It was "*literally*" on the other side of the tracks — an elevated train track separated the higher middle class from the lower middle class section with hand-writing on the iron bridge saying "*You are now entering Lil Chicago.*" Guess which side my family ended up?)

I also wrote for classes I presented to basic training recruits where I received commendations. The awards were more for the presentation than for my writing. But, I could not have done it had I not wrote my material. (This would do me well as a trial attorney when writing closing arguments and presenting 'em to a hundred different juries in Philadelphia.)

I remember having to write a letter for a young soldier who died in a car accident while serving as clerk in our training camp while in Ft. Polk, Louisiana. He had cheated on his wife, but I overlooked that in writing to his spouse, and spoke more about his feelings for her and the kids when I included the letter in a box we sent her containing his personal belongings.

Also, had to study and take notes for prosecuting several young soldiers who ran afoul of military life by going AWOL and/or disobeying orders. Did not like arguing before a summary court-martial, particularly when I won and felt it was my fault one of the defendants had to be punished. I knew him. And liked him. A fellow from New Orleans who just could not adjust to a regimented way of life. "*Don't take it so hard, Lt. Contos,*" the private told me after I apologized for having to "*bring him to justice.*" "*It's not your fault. I was the one that got me into this mess.*"

Military life played a major role in my other great summer job. As a Third-Year student out of Temple Law School I represented criminal defendants charged with failing to appear (FTA) in Court. They got bench warrants and had to appear before a judge or what we called a *"trial commissioner"* for a hearing to explain their *"no-show."* The worse cases were those at trial for the most serious cases, which we called *"Judge Only"* hearings, in which a defendant went before a *"sitting judge"* and not a trial commissioner, who may not even be a lawyer. (Like many of the *"Justices of the Peace"* who conducted initial judicial proceedings with the power to imprison and set bail, a trial commissioner could not decide guilt or innocence for a crime punishable by more than six months in jail. The Sixth Amendment to the US Constitution grants defendant, among other things, the right to a trial by judge *"and a jury."*

You were placed in custody once you showed up for a *"Judge Only'* bench warrant hearing. Chances were, you already had a record and were *"ducking"* Court, and not staying away for some legitimate reason. The time in custody would count toward an eventual sentence should it require your incarceration.

"Judge Only's" were the toughest to defend. Always seemed like we'd get before the meanest judge on the bench. Never saw many lawyers getting their clients off without some jail time, let alone hear of any interns *"winning"* an argument.

And, so it was when this down-on-his luck Vietnam era veteran appeared before Judge Michael Stiles, a Philadelphia Common Pleas Court judge who would later be appointed to serve with the Attorney Generals' Office under the Clinton administration. He had a reputation of being tough, but fair, having come up through the ranks, so to speak, while serving as a prosecutor before donning the black robes. He knew advocacy from the ground on up!

It had been several years since my client had failed to appear. Luckily, it was the only FTA. But, he did not have "ties" to Philadelphia, having just been released from Chester County, some 30 miles away where he was an inpatient at Coatesville (PA) VA (Veterans Administration) Medical Center. (Treated for alcohol-related problems, having never saw combat . . . [*I never revealed that part to the judge.*])

"Here's a man, who served in the Army . . . a Vietnam era veteran," I told the judge, using the *"correct"* terminology for such a non-combat veteran. *"Your Honor, he voluntarily admitted himself into the VA hospital, where he is now getting full-time treatment. He had to take a train and several buses to get to our city . . . He got here on time, and while we have no excuse for what he did, I submit to you he is a different man today than what he was facing you before. I ask you to take all of this into consideration for your decision."*

Judge Stiles cut off all speech the assistant district attorney (ADA) assigned to his court room was about to make. The ADA, a seasoned attorney, was expected to argue against me, a lowly intern, more than a year away from taking the bar exam to practice law.

The jurist spoke with the Wisdom of Solomon. I have no idea what he said, I was too exhausted following my rather emotional appeal for a fellow veteran. All I remember is that the warrant was *"lifted"* and my client given a new subpoena to appear in Court without being sent to jail. I'd later learn that many judges would give credit for *"time served"* for any legitimate inpatient program to rehabilitate a person. I like to think the man avoided jail and turned his life around, but public defenders hardly get a chance for follow-up work, having to deal with literally thousands of defendants over a 20-year career.

I think my two summer jobs served me well and helped form the person you see before you. Did the job make the man? Or the man make the job? You make the call.

Revenge could change, once 'you' change

NEVER THOUGHT *"REVENGE"* HAD ANYTHING good to say about itself. It's a negative trait. Falls in with Anger, Rage and *"getting even."*

But, what if one can use the *"energy"* that revenge supplies? What if it could be the catalyst to get someone out of their *"comfort zone"* and on to a new direction in life, starting out with a bad intent, but finishing up with something good, a *"right"* and meritorious deed?

That may have happened to me when bypassed for a promotion while a journalist. I was a decent reporter. Nothing special, even though my work involving the mentally retarded was nominated for a Pulitzer Prize.

I was a work horse who didn't mind digging, or sifting through government and financial documents to prove malfeasance and possible corruption in government offices as well as institutions run by the state and private industry.

Couldn't spell a lick. Discovered the art of *"headline writing"* only recently in having to create 'em for this Blog. In addition, the guy with less experience who got promoted from the ranks of reporter to copy editor was more articulate, could spell better, and served as a *"Nader Raider,"* one who worked in Washington, DC, with the internationally recognized consumer crusader, Ralph Nader. Could not begrudge him.

But, I was hurt. I wanted some recognition other than newspaper awards and thank-you letters. A copy editor made more money due primarily to *The Newspaper Guild* (TNG) which formed a union at *The Mercury* newspaper of Pottstown, PA.

That's where I sought my revenge.

I threw myself into union activities. Already served as the *"shop steward"* for the reporters, copy editors and photographers on staff. Had taken part in several contract negotiations, where I was the lone hold-out, often insuring the lowest-paid and often overlooked workers got a fair piece of the *"pie,"* the contract increases.

Not sure if I became president of our local unit in Pottstown before or after the job promotion incident. But you could not have asked for better timing unless you were writing a book.

I aided management in getting rid of some *"dead wood"* our union had supported in the past. Agreed to let a person go with *"three strikes and you're out"* when he showed up late for work a third time in a row. That's lack of respect for the job and the employer, I felt. Didn't need a Samuel Gompers (the *founder of the AF of L – the American Federation of Labor*) to tell me otherwise. (Note: Gompers worked with the US government during World War I to prevent strikes while increasing wages for workers. One hand, in deed, can often help the other, if both extend from sincere hearts.)

Gained respect from the advertising, circulation and business departments. Believe I showed the department heads the union would not abide by some practices and ensured adherence to the contract.

But, my greatest achievement was outside the paper, owned by the Ingersoll chain, a group of investors which included <u>Mark Goodson</u>, of American television's *Goodson-Toddman* game show empire.

With the help of TNG's Philadelphia Local secretary, I organized the *Ingersoll Council*, made up of 10 or more newspapers mostly on the East Coast, with a few in areas like Detroit, Michigan; Terre Haute, Indiana; as well as in California.

Inviting union leaders from each paper, we'd meet in Philadelphia, comparing notes of working conditions, salaries and "*past practices.*" I learned that "*past practice*" was a key to keeping job improvements a written contract was often silent about.

It was in the newsletters I wrote that I might have made the biggest impact. I got statistics on the hiring practices of women and blacks. For instance, The Delaware County (PA) newspaper, the largest in the chain, had but one African-American on its payroll. And he was a janitor. The paper covered areas bordering Philadelphia where the African-American population was growing and increasing weekly.

There was an unbelievable "*pay gap*" between women working on display ads versus classified ads. Learned this existed throughout the chain, and was prevalent at one time at the larger newspapers like the *Philadelphia Inquirer* and the *Philadelphia Daily News*, also represented by the Guild.

Got offered a new job by the Guild and took a leave of absence from *The Mercury newspaper* of Pottstown. Traveled Pennsylvania, New Jersey and Delaware roads as a union organizer, spreading the "*gospel*" of the labor movement, coming close to organizing units in Atlantic City, NJ, as well as Reading, PA, where more than enough cards were to signed call for a union election, only to meet with defeat when management in Reading hired "*union-busting*" consultants to offer it advise.

Got inspired to go to Law School and become a labor lawyer. Changed directions on getting a grade of "*D*" in Labor Law, and became a criminal attorney after getting a straight "*C+ average*" in all my criminal law classes.

Oh, almost forgot about the revenge factor.

The newspaper chain brought in a new publisher to run *The Mercury*. The new guy swept house, firing most of the department heads I had "*locked horns*" with more than a year earlier. He fired the editor of the paper, the only one I knew over a 10-year period, and the one in charge when no promotion was offered to me. Learned recently that Ralph <u>Ingersoll</u> II, who created one of America's largest private newspaper companies, sold his interest 20 years ago, according to the *Washington Post.* Happened just a few years after I curtailed my union work on his "*chain.*"

Did my revenge have anything to do with it? Would I have stayed content as a reporter, and not seek a position to possibly lead others to a better life?

Never thought I'd become a lawyer. Maybe that's part of the revenge of the cosmos, to place me in a group that a Shakespearean character said world would be better off without: "*. . . The first thing we do, let's kill all the lawyers.*" — ***Henry VI***

Failure can often lead to a greater success

I TOOK A LEAVE OF absence from my work as a newspaper reporter to serve as a union organizer for The Newspaper Guild of Philadelphia many years ago. I had helped to negotiate several contracts at my local newspaper in Pottstown, and only took the job when I was overlooked for being made a copy-editor at the paper.

Spelling and grammar were never my greatest skills and the guy they promoted was a lot better than me in both categories. It hurt never the less, and I guess I used that sense of failure to search for another outlet for the few skills I had developed.

I surprised myself in agreeing to take the job as a union organizer with no experience under my belt save a few songs I seemed to recall about the labor movement. (Woodie Guthrie comes to mind and so does the song about Joe Hill!)

I failed at the one and only National Labor Relations Board election I was able to piece together out of some 25 papers I canvassed over a year-long period. The election was held in Reading for the joint newspapers made up of The Times and the Eagle. It hurt badly to lose and I used that feeling to go to law school and get a degree to help the union movement and the working class people that I grew up with in Philadelphia. I wanted to become a labor lawyer.

Surprise, I got a D in labor law!

Once again, I used that hurt feeling to seek another avenue for a new career and I went into criminal law, figuring I'd be comfortable with the those types of miscreants, several of whom I had grown up with. I became a public defender, once representing a fellow from Brewerytown that once got into a fight with and continuously bad-mouthed my oldest brother. I represented that fellow to the best of my ability despite my loathing for him and the crime he was accused of committing.

I went on to complete a 20-year-career at the Philadelphia Defender Association, trying more than a hundred jury trials and winning more than half of them. I felt I finally found my true calling after so many different paths along my journey.

It's funny how a sense of failure can spur a person on to accomplish something completely different in one's life. One could believe there is a divine guidance in the Universe if one just opened to it.

A sense of failure doesn't seem so bad looking back nowadays.

Joe Hill never died, he went on to organize!

On this Labor Day weekend, I'd like to offer the song "Joe Hill" to all my union-supporting friends, and share the story of the man who helped me as a union organizer in what seem another lifetime ago.

Joe Hill came to the United States from Sweden and worked on railroads and in the mines. He joined the IWW, the Industrial Workers of the World (known as the "Wobblies") in hopes to unionize all workers for a better living wages and conditions.

He wrote songs and poems, which were published throughout the states. They included "The Preacher and the Slave" (in which he created the phrase "pie in the sky"), "The Tramp", "There is Power in a Union", "The Rebel Girl", and "Casey Jones—the Union Scab", which expressed the harsh but combative life of itinerant workers, and call for workers to organize their efforts to improve working conditions. Of all workers.

Hill was convicted of two murders in a controversial trial. Following an unsuccessful appeal, political debates, and international calls for clemency from high-profile figures and workers' organizations, Hill was executed in November 1915.

After his death, he was memorialized by several folk songs, including the one below, which Joan Baez sang at Woodstock in 1969. I listened to it when I was organizing newspapers in the mid-1980s in Reading, Pa, Atlantic City, NJ, and in West Chester, Pa, and I always got a chill, particularly when Joe Hill says what they couldn't kill "***went on to organize***."

Give a listen!

Joe Hill

A song by Alfred Hayes, Music by Earl Robinson©1938 by Bob Miller, Inc.

I dreamed I saw Joe Hill last night
Alive as you or me
Says I, But Joe, you're ten years dead
I never died, says he
I never died, says he

In Salt Lake, Joe, says I to him
Him standing by my bed
They framed you on a murder charge
Says Joe, But I ain't dead
Says Joe, But I ain't dead

The copper bosses killed you, Joe
They shot you, Joe, says I
Takes more than guns to kill a man
Says Joe, I didn't die
Says Joe, I didn't die

And standing there as big as life
And smiling with his eyes
Joe says, What they forgot to kill
Went on to organize
Went on to organize

Joe Hill ain't dead, he says to me
Joe Hill ain't never died
Where working men are out on strike
Joe Hill is at their side
Joe Hill is at their side

From San Diego up to Maine
In every mine and mill
Where workers strike and organize
Says he, You'll find Joe Hill
Says he, You'll find Joe Hill

I dreamed I saw Joe Hill last night
Alive as you or me
Says I, But Joe, you're ten years dead
I never died, says he
I never died, says he

**Professor James Strazzella presenting Michael J Contos (at right) with
the award for trial advocacy at Temple Law School in Philadelphia**

The Law taught to me by James Strazzella!

My CRIMINAL LAW PROFESSOR DIED and I cried like a baby on learning the news. I couldn't help but look at the photograph taken of him presenting me with a trial advocacy award upon graduation in 1988. The framed photograph rests on the mantel place above an old wood-burning stove in my dining room. It is one of my favorite keepsakes.

> *Professor James Strazzella made you think of the law and how the Constitution was a living document that grows through the years and grants rights to all by ensuring the rights for those accused of crimes.*

James Strazzella was acting dean of Temple Law School when I worked for him making $5.25 an hour as a work study student my senior year. I could never figure out how he chose a C+ student as an assistant when he could have had the pick of the best and the brightest A+ student at the Philadelphia school. It wasn't the "letter" of the law he was concerned with, however, but the "spirit" and I guess he saw something in a fellow whose immigrant father never made it beyond 6th grade but instilled in his son of love of learning and the American Dream to help others less fortunate than oneself.

I applied it to my practice for 20 years and feel that working with the law was more of a "calling" than a job. "*Strazz*" as we called him, wanted his students to revere the law and to know it was created by man to serve man for the good of all. I tried to keep that in mind when appearing before a jury that was formed to determine the outcome of a person's life and liberty. I am happy to say the system works just as my old professor instructed us it would in the courtrooms of the world.

God keep you Professor Strazzella . . . See you in your next life's incarnation!

Michael J

'12 Angry Men' helps presume innocence

"TWELVE ANGRY MEN" INFLUENCED MY decision to practice law more than any movie I remember while growing up in Philadelphia and being the first in my family to go to college. The movie has done more for showing the workings of the criminal justice system than any books or school classes could possibly provide.

> I never liked lawyers. They reminded me of snakes -- something to avoid if you ever came across one. My father retained a blind lawyer to represent my oldest brother when he and others from Brewerytown broke into the Big Moose bar and stole cases of soda and beer. The attorney plea-bargained and got the judge to agree to let my brother choose between going into the army and going to jail. He went into the military, got his GED and made a 20-year career out of it.

But I became a lawyer to represent workers, union employees after serving a year as a union and getting a "D" in Labor Law while in law school. I took the grade as a message from God to change my "major" and went into criminal law where I worked for the poor who could not afford a spokesman when they were over-charged and sometimes charged erroneously for alleged criminal activities.

Trying a case to a jury was thrilling. You didn't eat, sleep or function properly during the trial as your mind and heart took on one single goal – defending the accused. Luckily, I won more than I lost. It would only take one person on a jury to convince the others to vote not guilty. Just one person was all it took to use my arguments in court to sway the others due to the lack of any substantial evidence.

And just like a Henry Fonda, the hero of the movie, that lone juror would not quit on the accused. He or she would point out the weaknesses in the prosecutor's case and remind each and every last member that it was burden of the state's lawyer to prove guilt. The defense had no burden, and if the assistant district attorney could not prove guilt beyond a reasonable doubt then you had to acquit.

Find the defendant not guilty as in the movie after a rigorous argument about the facts or lack of the facts, which often proved fatal to the state's case.

I never served on jury, but I envisioned what it would be like by watching "Twelve Angry Men." It's a movie that should be shown to all potential jurors but I'm afraid that prosecutors and judges may deny its presentation for fear of tilting the playing field in favor of an accused who some still believe should be presumed innocent until proven guilty.

A Jury can 'nullify' a law to stop injustice

Jury nullification.

Mandatory sentence.

As a lawyer in at least one country I am aware, I would not be permitted to speak to you of the above two terms should you happen to be serving on a jury.

See, the government of the United States thought it wiser to keep that information away from a jury hearing a trial in a criminal case. Some jurors might want to take the law into their own hands, so to speak.

That's what jury nullification actually is. A jury has the power to "*nullify*" a law it does not want to follow. Understand that? If you feel the law would be unjust, you can simply decide not to apply the law.

Can anyone spell anarchy? That's what would happen if every jury sworn in to uphold the law took it upon itself to disregard it. But, I'm not talking about every case. Just the exceptional one where 12 people agree that application of the law would cause more harm than good.

Kinda goes along with mandatory sentences. Defense lawyers in this same country are not permitted to tell a jury that its verdict will lead to mandatory outcomes, no matter what a jury might have been lead to believe. Studies show that most juries believe defendants usually end up getting probation or some "*light*" sentence. But state legislators in this country wanted to insure no "*lenient*" judge could get away with not "*sending someone away*" no matter what the circumstances for certain offenses.

A lot of "mandatory" sentences have to do with crimes against victims of a certain age. Do you know if you strike a child of a certain age, the law mandates that you serve at least one year in jail, no matter what? Unless a prosecutor agrees to "*demandatorize*" a sentence, a babysitter 18 or older slapping a child of a certain age must serve 365 days in jail upon conviction, at least in the part of the country I'm talking about.

A young man who is led to believe the young female he spent the night with was over a certain age, faces a similar mandatory sentence. It's called statutory rape, no matter what lies the person under 14 offered, or the lack of intent to commit any crime when he had consensual sex.

Most may say the sombitch deserves it. Unless it is a member of their family, a close friend, or, God forbid, *themselves.*

Or got involved with drugs and had on your possession an amount that presupposes possession with the intent to deliver, which calls for, you guessed it, a mandatory sentence no matter what the circumstances.

I was shocked when I learned a person who simply possessed a certain amount of marijuana could be charged with a felony for selling dope. People I knew in my teens often purchased an ounce or more. If they'd put the grass in small zip lock bags for later use and or convenience, the packaging of the marijuana itself could lead to rebuttable presumption it was for the "*intent to deliver.*"

Well, a jury could disregard the law if it saw fit.

But I was never allowed to tell a jury in Philadelphia that it had such power. Not permitted to even mention mandatory sentence or I'd face contempt charges from a judge. Sentencing is not in the *"province"* of the jury, only guilt or innocence, is what a judge would instruct me after my imprisonment, monetary fine, or both.

Could not tell a jury in America that landmark cases such as those involving William Penn, the founder of Pennsylvania, or John Peter Zenger, a New York printer whose case stood for both freedom of the press and truth as a defense against libel, were kept from imprisonment because a jury saw fit to disregard the law each brave man had so clearly broken. They were found *"Not Guilty,"* despite the law. Some might say *"in spite"* of the law.

A dream I had last night inspired me to whisper this piece of advice to you should you ever serve on a jury. Go ahead. Disregard the law if you, in all *"good consciousness"* feel it's the right thing to do.

It really is the American Way no matter what my government won't allow me to tell you.

Courtroom awakens karma understanding

ONE OF THE MOST HUMBLING times in my life occurred in Court.

Philadelphia Police Sgt. Washington motioned to me that he wanted to talk. This was odd, I represented the "*other side*" as public defender whose client was the defendant charged in an auto theft case. Washington was the arresting police officer whose testimony would insure a conviction.

"*You from Philadelphia?*" this muscular African-American police officer asked me in a quiet tone. Another case had been called to the bar of the Court and we stood in the audience away from the attorney tables.

"*I grew up in Philly, North Philly. Why?*" I said, wondering what I had done wrong. Always get that feeling when talking with police. Old Catholic guilt, I guess.

"*We used to live on the same block,*" he said, and taught me something I hope I never forget.

"*You helped me learn how to read.*"

I was taken back. Looking closer at this man, I tried but failed to recognize him. I searched memory banks of the homes I lived at, and the friends I had both in and out of school. No luck.

Until, the sergeant mentioned Marston St. — 1434 N. Marston Street -- to be exact. Less than a block away from St Ludwig's Roman Catholic Church and elementary school. *"You're that Washington?"* I said, as a beam of light shone and I remembered a skinny little Black kid who would sit on the steps outside the house as I did my "extra" homework for my Third Grade teacher, a nun who was forcing me to learn the "Palmer Method" of handwriting. My handwriting was so bad, this senile Franciscan nun with the thickest pair of bifocals I had ever seen, thought she could improve it through repetitive scrawling on my part. She was wrong. About the *"hand-writing."* (Maybe she saw something in my *"writing"* that she wanted to straighten out before I'd get the chance to utter something blasphemous or profane in the eyes of God? Could she see into my future?)

I'd handwrite one letter after another, trying my best not to bend my wrist but allow each symbol to evolve with a fluid motion. Got that? Well, neither did I. One of the purposes of the Palmer Method was to help someone to write and write some more without tiring out the hand, or causing the repetitive strain we see computer typists suffering from today.

But there I was, my legs drawn up, back hunched over a loose-leaf folder, scribbling away as the young Washington fellow approached and asked what I was up to. I showed him, try to explain it, and welcomed the chance take a break from such tedious work. At some point, he must have brought out his homework and I remember going over it with him. Hey, I was pretty smart as a Third-Grader. Had no interest in girls or sports and had the fear of God instilled in me by fearless nuns I hardly ever had time or the inclination to sin. I studied. The alternative could have been hell.

I must have helped the fellow who was some two years younger than me. We'd meet outside my house day after day, him with his reading book and me with my writing one. I enjoyed helping him. I see now that he may have gotten more out of the excursions than anyone would think possible. *I helped him realize he had the ability within to read.*

He helped me to realize that actions, no matter how small, could have an immensely unproportioned effect on another. And I felt humbled when the Universe enlightened me of this karmic cause and effect.

The courtroom case was continued for some reason, and I shook hands with Sgt. Washington hoping our paths would cross again. They will, if the cause and conditions arise for us again.

Jury Trial Faced My First Day on the Job

You gotta be careful for what you wish for . . .

Your dream just might come true. Over . . . and over . . . and over again.

Like trying a case to a jury my first day in the Major Trial Division of Philadelphia's common pleas court system . . .

For two years, I was biting at the bit to showcase my few legal skills before 12 jurors deciding the guilt or innocence of a criminal defendant. I was among the last of 15 new attorneys hired by the Defender Association of Philadelphia, the city's public defender office, to get a chance at jury trial practice.

It took me longer to learn the legal profession lingo. Heck, I had trouble with English, let alone the Latin terms needed to influence a judge with how much jurisprudence I knew. By the time I got to Major Trials, more than half the Class of 1988 was advising me on what to expect for the trial, and the procedure leading up to "*demanding*" a jury to hear a case for the first time in my legal career. (Before finishing a 20-year-stint, I'd "*demand*," and would try, more than a *hundred jury cases* — once doing 10 jury trials in the span of nine weeks, an informal record at the PD office.)

Demand is the correct word, by the way. A criminal defendant facing more than six months in jail has an automatic right under the US Constitution to assert his or her right to trial by jury. God bless our forefathers. Most people never need to face a *"jury of their peers,"* unless chosen to *serve* at the county or federal government levels.

In Philadelphia, all the more serious cases were earmarked by Court administration for *"Major Felony"* treatment. That is, for a possible jury trial. Cases involving less serious felonies were scheduled in the *"waiver"* program. They were cases legal professionals believed would be tried to a judge sitting without a jury when a defendant would *"waive"* the right to a jury trial. Hence, the term *"waiver"* trial.

Many lawyers prefer waiver trials, also known as *"bench"* trials where one person learned in the law — a judge — renders a verdict. It takes less time, preparation and overall wear and tear on a lawyer to try a case to a judge than to a jury, and some of Philadelphia's best trial attorneys have been known to avoid jury trials like the plague.

Not me. It was the main reason I went into the practice of law. That is, after getting a "D" in a Labor Law class and took it as a sign from God to seek a different field to specialize. *(I got a C-Plus in my Criminal Law classes!)* Jury practice offered me a chance to act before a captured audience and to get people to like me. Actually, to get 'em to like my version of the facts presented them over a four or five-day jury trial.

That's about the average time for such a procedure, including the *"Voir Dire"* where the defense attorney and a prosecuting attorney get a chance to ask each potential juror questions to determine any biases. We'd choose a jury of 12 and two alternates from a *"panel"* of 40 people, rejecting a few for various reasons. Picking a jury would take a full day on the average. An uncomplicated case could be tried in two or three days, with deliberations taking anywhere from 15 minutes (shortest I ever experienced), to several days. Some ended after jurors became *"hung,"* that is, were unable to reach a unanimous verdict, and the judge declared a mistrial.

But the chances of a new attorney "*demanding*" and trying a jury case his first day "*on the job*," so to speak, were slim and hardly ever heard of 20 years ago. Unless you had my luck. And then you ended up with one of Philadelphia's worst judges — worst for the defense — your first time up to bat.

(See Part II next)

All's well that ends well with a Not Guilty

SOMETIMES WHILE TRYING A CASE, a transformation would take place when I least expected it. I'd begin to believe my criminal client had been truthful when he told me he was innocent.

That's what happened in my first jury trial in 1990. Tried a case before Judge L, a crotchety old buzzard for whom no one would "*waive*" a case because he had no reasonable doubt. He was one of six or seven judges in Philadelphia defense lawyers dreaded to face with a close case, one that a more moderate judge could go either way with a verdict. I could not trust this judge to be fair, mostly because of the countless number of cases he heard, and the many creative "*defenses*" criminal defense lawyers exposed him to. He heard 'em all.

So, I was "*stuck*" with trying to a jury whether I wanted to or not!

I know of only one other lawyer in the Philadelphia Defender Association that ever did a jury trial his first day in "*Majors.*" Mark Wilson, an attorney with the federal public defender's office in Philadelphia. He and I were the only ones out of hundreds of us serving in the more than 50-year history of the Philly PD's Office to "*get up to bat*" our very first day in the "*Majors.*"

In most cases, new lawyers would go weeks, sometimes months, even years before doing their first jury trial. They'd watch pros in action and learn the craft from both sides, the defense and the prosecution. You'd have two to three months to bring a case to jury trial, before being *"rotated"* out of Majors and into the *"Waiver"* courtrooms where cases were tried to judges sitting alone without juries, generally, the less serious and less complicated ones. Our office *"rotated"* attorneys in and out of Majors to give the new PDs their chance to finally get in front of a jury.

I never expected on my first day to be *"sent out"* from Courtroom 625, which served as the court system's *"staging area,"* to pick a jury elsewhere in Philadelphia's City Hall building. I walked to the bar of the Court when my client's case was called. It was a *"first listing"* with no previous continuances. All cases *"older in time"* were put on hold when their lawyers could not be located. I later learned some lawyers — even the best ones — would *"continue"* cases (some might say *"duck"* a case) when a *"bad"* judge (a prosecutorial-leaning judge) would become the only one available to hear a case. If the names of certain judges were called (can anyone say Angelo Guarino, removed from the bench in the middle of a trial for violating the rights of a potential juror?) you could not *"waive"* but had to request a jury. Professional ethics mandated you demand such a trial to safeguard you client's interest. Either that, or get a good deal to plead guilty.

The trial went smoothly and *"broke my way"* as the main witness admitted under cross-examination he had only a limited view of my client when he saw a group of similarly dressed persons take part in a crime (drug sale). At that point, I actually started to believe my client may not have committed the crime. I believe it showed in my closing argument. I later learned that a good lawyer would often reserve judgment of a client's guilt, but may come to believe in a "possibility of" innocence when facts — or the lack of facts — arose at trial. It became part of my *"trial mode."*

The jury agreed with me –that the assistant district attorney's witness could have been *"mistaken."* They were not convinced of the defendant's guilt. And they rendered a not guilty verdict.

"I didn't want to tell you during the actual trial, but now I can let you know: this is my first jury trial," I whispered to my client as we sat at the defense table after the announced verdict. The defendant, who was in his late 30s and not the age of your typical drug dealer, but with a record for old *"assault and batteries,"* leaned toward me, his hand on my shoulder and said with all innocence, *"my first one, too."*

Smoke handcuffs me when stress hits home

I NEVER WANTED A CIGARETTE as bad as I did when I got thrown into a "lockup" after getting kicked out of the courtroom by a judge whose ire I had raised by raising my own voice at him.

There I stood in an 8-by-10 foot cell room with a metal bench and a thick glass in which I could see someone enter in a cramped walkway outside to speak with me. No one appeared as I looked out into empty space, asking myself if it was worth it. Why did I raise my voice at the judge? I got kicked out of another courtroom for the same outrage, but survived a contempt of court sanction when my office switched me from one judge to this other one for following the same procedure against a loudmouth like yours truly.

What I wouldn't give for a smoke, I thought. No, it was more of a feeling, a longing, and a desperate yearning for that satisfying first and second puff that could assure me that I'd get through yet another fine mess I got myself into.

I had quit smoking some seven years earlier. Went cold turkey. It occurred when I was trapped in a dentist chair and I wanted a ciga-rette to get me through the procedure and I knew I couldn't light up. I applied what I believe was "mind over matter," and it got me through the procedure. I might have actually meditated without knowing it, as I curbed my thoughts of such an agonizing discomfort. All I did was breathe slowly and not think of anything while the dentist moved his hands and instruments from one tooth to another inside my big mouth.

I emptied my mind of the desire for all desire to smoke.

And it worked. The next time I wanted to catch a smoke, I put *"mind over matter"* again. It wasn't easy. Ask any anyone who ever quit. It was worse when I'd find myself in situations where I'd normally shake out one of my Marlboro Lights and light it up. Like the first cup of coffee in the morning. (With no breakfast, mind you!)

Or after having sex and lighting up before falling asleep on my back. Smoking was great after a really good meal, and I'd also have a good smoke while singing with my Doo Wop street corner singing group in Brewerytown, a section of North Philadelphia.

But there I was, dying for a smoke, if you know what I mean. Smoking was ingrained in me as a youngster. Both parents smoked; my dad liked Chesterfield and my mom Pall Mall (Neither had filters.) I took up the habit at the tender age of twelve and didn't stop for some 30 years.

When I finally did, I'd have dreams of cigarettes. They were sensual in nature and I'd wake up in a cold sweat after 'em.

I could have cared less for sex then, for the only thing that could have satisfied me was a couple of drags from a smoke, be it a Camel or even a Lucky Strike. All would be well with the world again.

My craving ended when a lawyer from the Defender Association appeared before the judge, plead my "temporary insanity," and chalked it up to my being overly zealous, something the judge himself knew all too well, and he imposed no further penalty.

At that time, all I wanted was a good stiff drink to celebrate my freedom. And I would have given my life for it at that moment, if you know what I mean.

Honesty always the best policy in her court

You should never call a woman a bitch.

Particularly if she's wearing a long black robe and has the power to throw you in jail for anything deemed to be contempt of court. Her court, that is.

Worse yet, however, is not to be truthful with the tribunal. I learned this the hard way. Call it a lesson from the School of Hard Knocks.

I had been assigned to the courtroom of the Honorable Genece E. Brinkley for about a month when I found myself defending a defendant on her probation. During the violation hearing, the probation officer told the judge my client had not paid any money towards his restitution and failed to come to the probation office as required.

I cross-examined the officer, an attractive African-American woman, and got placed onto the record the facts that the defendant had recently gotten a job in a county outside of Philadelphia and that he took public transportation to the workplace each day. He had not completed his 90 day probationary period with the job, and felt he couldn't take time off to see his probation officer in person.

In addition, the court officer had to admit that the defendant had made payments to the court system, but that all moneys initially went toward court costs and not to restitution. That could be hundreds of dollars, in some cases.

The judge wanted to revoke his bail and send him back to jail, but she relented, placing him on house arrest with permission to go to work from his residence.

"You gotta be truthful when you're dealing with a goddam bitch like this judge" I scolded the probation officer when we had left the courtroom and stood in the crowded hallway of Philadelphia's Criminal Justice Center. I told her that she should have told the judge the good things my client had done along with what she considered to be the bad.

The next thing I knew, I was being called into the judge's chambers about a half hour later. The judge had her law clerk contact my office and I learned one of my supervisor's was enroute to see the judge. Along with me.

"I heard you called me a bitch" Judge Brinkley said looking me dead in the eyes as we convened in the jurist's "robing room."

I blinked once or twice, looking at the probation officer who I later learned had sought out the judge and told her about my discussion outside of court. The probation officer had been sitting next to a prosecutor who I never got along with, one I never could trust, if you know what I mean.

"No your honor," I said, looking the judge in the eyes." I called you a 'goddam' bitch."

My supervisor nearly fell out of his chair saying nothing as he continually shook his head in what looked like denial.

"I think you are sexist, Mr. Contos. If I were a male judge, you never would have used that term," Judge Brinkley said, her eyes once again never leaving mine as if she could see into my very soul.

"You're right, you honor," I addressed her with her title once again.

"If you were a male judge," I said, once again using her honorific title. "I'd probably call you a prick!"

I don't know for sure, but I believe a slight smile crossed the judge's face at that moment. She said nothing for several long moments as I awaited my fate. Finally, she dismissed me and nothing else was said, as she discharged the assistant district attorney – another woman — and the probation officer.

Nothing ever came of that incident except for a great little war story I can tell about honesty always being the best policy. Even if you're threatened with contempt of court and a possible fine or imprisonment.

Philadelphia Justice with Judge Lineberger

MY ALL-TIME FAVORITE PHILADELPHIA JUDGE was James Lineberger, a no-nonsense jurist who'd scare the hell out of many a defendant I'd bring to the bar of the court, and one time caused one of my clients to pass out when he sentenced him for a heinous crime a jury found him guilty of committing.

Judge Lineberger could also be as warm and fuzzy as a teddy bear who would leave the bench at the top of the courtroom and float down to the metal bar when spotting a Korean woman. He could serenade in her native tongue while gazing out from his big lovable and loving eyes.

The judge was also a US army veteran, the only one I ever met who received a battlefield commission – being elevated from the ranks of an "enlisted man" to that of an officer when he served with utmost distinction in the Vietnam War. He served more than 20 years in "this man's army," and then went to law school before working for the Philadelphia District Attorney's Office under Ed Rendell who would later become mayor of our fair city and then governor of the State of Pennsylvania.

I met Mr. Lineberger, Esquire, at another point of his majestic career. He served as a criminal defense lawyer and took on a jurist who I detested and – I hate to say this – "hated" while that man served as judge in the Common Pleas Courts of Philadelphia. That judge got into a heated discussion with Lineberger who never once backed down or gave an inch. The jurist (Ah hell

— his name was Angelo Guarino) raised his loud Italian voice and shouted *"Do you know who you're talking to?"*

The six-foot, four-inch African American Lineberger never batted an eyelash when he replied; "Do you know who *you're* talking to?"

Attorney-at-law Lineberger represented many Koreans during his private practice. Many were from what I learned was the Korean section of Philadelphia. He learned much of the language while serving in the military.

I'm get ready to visit the DMZ (Demilitarized Zone) here in Korea. I don't believe that it was an accident in meeting a man so in love with this country. I think the Universe offered a foreshadowing of what was to come for me more than a decade later.

I once represented a drummer for a famous Philadelphia Rock & Roll band that had been inducted into the Rock & Roll Museum. He had fallen on hard times and had eventually found a hard way of living. Five or six other lawyers in the Defender Association of Philadelphia had "continued" his case knowing that it was what we called a "loser," and that they wanted him to remain on the streets for as long as possible before facing judgement day.

I never liked continuances, so I tried the case and he was found guilty. As I stood with him at the time of sentencing he took his punishment "like a man."

And then he fainted.

A court crier and a sheriff immediately rushed to his aid and someone got him a cup of water before he regained his footing. He was taken away in handcuffs to serve 15-to-30 years, a moderate sentence I thought for the crimes he was accused of and the pain he must have caused his victims – who were both members of his own family.

That was my second introduction to Mr. Lineberger, the former army captain and prosecutor. I was at the bar of the court when I witnessed his challenge to the judge many of the Philadelphia defense bar disliked because he tilted the "playing field" in favor of the prosecution. I admired him for his guts and courage to stand up to Judge Guarino. I, in the meantime set an unofficial public defender record by trying ten jury trials in nine weeks – nine of them in front of that feared, prosecutorial-leaning judge. (He was later removed from the bench by the order of the State Supreme Court for gross misuse of his power in treatment of Philadelphia citizens applying for "hardship" exemptions from serving on his juries. He was physically removed from the bench in the middle of a jury trial and escorted out of the courtroom while another judge too his place.

The third time I faced Judge Lineberger was when my office assigned me to his courtroom, where I tried cases for a full year as a public defender. It is from this position that I got a close up view of the man and felt such an affinity to and for him.

He was one of the fairest judges to try a case to. I believe any prosecutor would agree. I never tried a non-jury trial before him, that is, a trial without a jury. That in and of itself tells you something, and that is, he was not what some would call a "defense-oriented" judge. (Two of my other favorite judges were called defense oriented. They were former public defenders of whom I will ask to marry me when I find another wife in my next lifetime! Got that?)

I had never heard the term "Big-Headed Irishman" until Judge Lineberger referred to another jurist in Philadelphia with whom he had worked with at the Philadelphia DA's office, Judge Jeffrey Minehart. He said it in jest and admiration, the way true friends and close family members can call each other names because they are really terms of endearment

The ruggedly handsome Judge Lineberger was also a lady's man wearing nothing but the finest garbs money could buy. Hell, he was receiving several pensions by the time I met him as a jurist. The assistance came from Social Security, the army and the city for which he served as a prosecutor. How else could he have afforded to have personal attendants — several of whom were attractive women — visit him in his "cloaking" room to advise him on his wardrobe an, one can only assume, take measurements. He dressed immaculately and caught the eye of the young and old!

Yes, he also had an eye out for women. Once, I had requested the Spanish interpreter from the Defender's office join me and Judge Lineberger was all smiles as she translated what my client said during a plea arrangement. After she left, the judge beamed and said quite often that she was *"very pleasing to the eye."*

A woman figured greatly during one of only two times that I was ever thrown out of a courtroom. She was a rather sexy woman in her early 30s who had appeared in support of her Mafia-Wannabe South Philadelphian boyfriend who forced a retrial when his court-appointed lawyer displeased him and the defendant upended the defense table in the middle of the trial in full view of the jury.

I was appointed to represent him for his contempt of court hearing and met him in the courtroom's adjacent "lock-up" cell room. He was a dark skinned, dark-looking Italian fellow who spoke with a South Philly accent. Picture a Rocky Balboa, but a little smaller and a lot more of a smart-aleck. He didn't like his other lawyer because he was "no good" and "was losing the case" for him, he said. The attorney broke his glasses during the trial and rather than get a new pair, he taped the dark glasses together with a white strip of to hold the broken stem to the spectacle main frame.

"I offered to buy him a new pair, but he refused" the defendant told me. What caused him to go crazy was when the lawyer split his pants at the trial and the jurors saw his white underwear through the tear. It was then, he said, that he overturned the table and cursed out his barrister.

Leaving the defendant, I re-entered the courtroom. A lovely woman approached me and introduced herself as his fiancé. She was breathtaking to look at and very *"easy on the eye."* I tried to explain there was very little that could be done for her friend, but that I would try to do my best. (There were little if any chances the judge would ever lower bail or reduce the fine, but I didn't tell her that.)

Well, I gave it my best shot when the defendant was brought into court. Judge Lineberger nailed me every time I'd raise an argument. He was correct, but I kept trying to show my client — and more so his girlfriend — that I was fighting for him.

Judge Lineberger must have taken offense. He was having quite a discussion with the young lady when I asked him to take notice of her as part of my client's family. He made eyes at her, if you know what I mean. Any full-blooded American male would understand what I'm saying. And the judge wouldn't stand for some low-life of a lawyer like me trying to upstage him.

He ordered sheriffs to arrest me after I raised my voice too loudly.

He then called me the most hurtful name anyone ever uttered about me in a court of law:

"Take this . . . short . . . lawyer out of here!"

(Contos means *"short"* in some foreign language. I never did find out how he learned it. It hurt. I'm only five-foot, six inches!)

I don't know what happened to the defendant or his girlfriend. I was set free when a supervisor from my office came to court and plead my case. I was "zealously representing the interest of a client" the supervising lawyer said, adding that I must have stepped over the line. I believe I actually bowed to the judge when he declined to hold me in contempt and freed me from the situation.

It became one of the best "war stories" of my legal career, bar none!

But my favorite story involved a client charged with robbery outside of what I'd call a "girlie bar" in West Philadelphia. The assistant district attorney, a season homicide lawyer who was given a break with cases of a less serious nature, accused the defendant of gun-point robbery even though no gun was recovered. My client had a lot of hard cash on his person and it was used as evidence against him.

I simply told the client's story in a rather colorful way during the trial and ended up citing lyrics from an Oldie-but-a-Goodie Rock & Roll song called *"Stagger Lee."* Singer Lloyd Price spoke of two men *"gambling late."*

"Stagger Lee threw a seven. Billy swore he threw an eight."

They were shooting craps, the game of dice, in the song!

And that is exactly what my client told me truly happened. The so-called victim left the bar and gambled away his money with the defendant. Rather than admit his loss to his girlfriend, he claimed that he was robbed. He had not called the police until his girlfriend forced him to. (This was backed up by evidence, the police phone records.) I argued that he'd be kicked out if he told the truth and the jury bought it.

What sealed the deal, I believe, was when I "published" my client to the jury. I got permission from the judge for my client to take the witness stand for one and only one purpose only. He rolled down the sleeve of his arm and showed a bright red and blue tattoo on it.

It was a pair of dice showing two numbers, a three and a four. A seven — which turned out to be a real winner!

I'll never forget what Judge Lineberger said as the jury was dismissed and my client's family members hugged him and shook my hand following the not-guilty verdict.

As I was leaving, silence had descended onto the courtroom. The judge looked down upon me and recited part of the song with his deep bass voice "*Go Stagger Lee . . . Go!*" It was the best exit line I ever heard!

Impeachment turns a loser into a winner

EACH DAY FOR TWENTY YEARS, the spirit of Don Quixote welcomed me into my law office. This picture hung above my desk reminding me that it was the "*impossible cases*" a good public defender relished. The ones you didn't expect to win, but somehow, now and then, you'd convince a jury to see the facts your way, which in most cases, was the right way.

I'd try cases other attorneys would "*duck*" month after month, seeking continuances. Particularly when a defendant was "*on the street*" working or supporting himself whatever way our indigent clients could find. I always felt that the "*buck stops here*," when such a file appeared on my desk: the tough cases signaled the greatest challenges. I had nothing to lose as an advocate — but a great deal to gain. To "*practice*" a new and "*untried*" theory of defense. Or try an unorthodox way to shake up a system normally stacked against you, and make it more favorable for a client. And in losing, I'd sharpen my skill and hone my trade for a more "*triable*" case next time.

I won more than I lost of the 100 jury trials I tried. A few real "*losers,*" would take on a life of their own, as facts unbeknownst to the prosecutor and myself would leak from the witness stand, surfacing as an acquittal when the verdict was read.

I remember one in particular. A "*caught-inside*" burglary. Police arrested a defendant inside a mechanic's garage where the owner held my client at bay.

The owner swore he *"caught him in the act"* and held a bat on the defendant; facts showed he might have held him at gunpoint. Police said nothing was reported stolen; the complainant read a two-page list of losses to the jury. Police described the business site in the West Philadelphia neighborhood as a *"trouble"* spot; the owner testified to the complete opposite. The jury acquitted after finding the *"victim"* unworthy of belief who had over-reacted to *innocent*, and not *criminal* behavior. In essence, they found the defendant may well have been at this scene seeking a job at an adjoining junkyard accepting employment applications that early morning.

I loathed this type of case as a new lawyer, however. You're supposed to cross-examine witnesses at a preliminary hearing to *"lock"* them into their story, so they wouldn't be able to change it at a later trial without facing something called *"impeachment."* The impeachment process involved an attorney confronting a witness at a later trial with a prior recorded statement (or a statement by a so-called *"collaborating witness"*) totally different from the story they were now *"selling"* to a jury. The prior statement was recorded and transcribed by a court reporter. A good attorney would have almost memorized key details from the *"notes"* of the hearing, and *"sense"* when someone said something even slightly different about a critical fact in a case. (A damn good attorney could *inflate* the difference in competing statements, thereby *"creating"* an almost theatrical atmosphere to convince a jury the witness lied, or had no idea what they were talking about.) The *"caught-inside burglary"* was an impossible criminal case to defend. Unless some impeachment broke your way. And then the fun began:

> *"If they're mistaken about fact "A," how can you, the jury, be convinced "beyond a reasonable doubt" they're not mistaken about fact "B?" The prosecutor is asking you to decide when his witness is telling the truth. He (she) wants you to guess which version is correct.*

> *Well, this is not some game of chance. We're not playing slots in Atlantic City or Vegas. We're dealing with my client's liberty. You can't play*

games with that. I won't let you, and neither will your own conscience. Remember! You took an oath to uphold the law, not bend it like the prosecutor would have you do. And, so . . . I beg of you. Demand more . . . Then do the right thing. . . Find him Not Guilty!"

A cop who arrested my client for selling contraband got into an argument with a court reporter when I confronted him with what he had said earlier at a preliminary hearing. He testified the defendant had hidden a stash of drugs on the back fender of a car. At trial, he said it was the front fender. It was a mistake anyone of us could make, particularly if we're handling a hundred arrests between the time of the hearing and the moment of trial, which in Philadelphia would run an average of at least four or five months.

I walked him through his testimony, reminding the jury that he was under oath, swearing to tell the truth, and that a person was typing every single word, just as they were at the present trial. The cross-examination culminated with the following: *"Four months ago, you said it was the 'back' fender. Yet today, you tell this jury it was the 'front.' Isn't that correct?"*

I sat and asked nothing more. The police officer criticized the absent reporter. Bad-mouthed the person, as I *"egged"* him on, reading the name of the reporter of whom I knew, pointing out her ten-years of experience by way of peppered questions to the witness. Got the court reporter of *"real time"* into the act, by singling out her to the witness. *"You can't trust what any of them write,"* the police officer said. I let the long — almost deadly silence — sink in, before announcing *"no more questions."*

Up until that point, I thought my client was guilty. He might have been. But I *"got him off"* of a mandatory three-year-sentence for what was his first offense, and he owed it all to man who refused to admit he made a mistake, thereby creating doubt in the minds of the jury.

"Are you as sure about that fact as you are of every fact you presented to this jury?"

He sealed his own fate as soon as he said yes.

And the impossible dream came true.

Too afraid to say a woman scared you

"Why did you shoot her?"
"I don't know."

WITH THESE THREE WORDS, THE defendant buried himself, and no matter what I did to rehabilitate a self-defense claim before the jury, we were sunk. It showed that no matter what one plans, sometimes something can, and always will, go wrong.

The defendant in the jury trial had done well on direct examination as I walked him through the facts of the case. He testified that he was visiting the young woman's house to see her brother, someone we claimed was dealing drugs, albeit the minor contraband of marijuana. They had gotten into an argument that became physical and the brother knocked the defendant to the living room floor, spilling along with him money from drug sales that had covered a coffee table. While falling, my client had pushed the cushion of a love seat askew, revealing a small handgun we claimed the brother had hidden there.

The two men struggled for the exposed gun, with my client getting control. He fired the weapon when the assailant's older, but much smaller, sister rushed toward them to help her brother.

"Why did you shoot her?" the prosecutor posed on cross-examination. It was what is known as an open-ended question, and not a very good one. An attorney should never ask a question unless he or she knows what the answer will be.

"I don't know," the defendant answered just as badly. But, he said it with such honesty, the jury took notice.

It was the wrong thing to say. There was a ring of truth to it, and despite any reasons or explanations we could later offer, it sealed his conviction.

I had gone over his testimony again and again, stressing how he must convince the jury that he was fearful for his life, that the only reason he pulled the trigger was to defend against serious bodily injury. It was the classic response for an affirmative self-defense claim. You cannot use deadly force against another unless you believed such force was being used against you. It's called a justification defense. None of this sunk in, or if it had, my client had frozen and reverted to a child-like youngster who, while not meaning any harm, could not say he was scared by the girl, something the fact-finders needed to hear to render a "not guilty" verdict.

"She had come at me with something in her hand," the defendant had told me. He couldn't say what she held, be it a pen or a letter-opener. At the time of the shooting, he could not distinguish it from a more serious object, like a knife, which presented us with a decent self-defense argument. "I didn't mean to shoot her," he said. What I couldn't get this young person barely out of his teens to admit was that he was afraid of her while lying on the floor. He just couldn't say or mouth the words, "afraid," "fearful," or "scared." Was it macho on his part? Was he afraid to admit a tiny female could make him squirm like a baby? I don't know.

I hired an expert. The former coroner of a neighboring county testified to the angle of the gunshot wound and its trajectory. It was caused by a shot fired from below the victim, on an angle from where the defendant said he lay sprawled on the floor.

The prosecutor presented his own expert, who claimed the woman was shot from a different angle, thereby canceling out my expert, causing the jury to base its verdict solely on lay witness testimony.

I got close to crossing the line during the trial. Unable to bring out the record of her brother because of procedural rules, I got his mug shot, blew up the arrest photo, and stood with my back to the jury providing a full view of the picture when asking if she could identify the picture as that of her brother.

The prosecutor objected. The judge sustained the objection and ordered it kept out of the record as evidence.

The jury found my client guilty, the first and only time I lost a trial before this judge. He was known for imposing the maximum sentences. My client got twelve years, the maximum. It was his first offense.

His sentence, however, was thrown out following an appeal, and the defendant ended up having to serve six years, slightly more than what the prosecutor sought for a guilty plea for aggravated assault. That required a minimum sentence of five-to-10 years.

I heard nothing more about the woman or her brother. There were no permanent injuries, and as far as I know they could have gone on to live happily ever after.

I hope the years have taught my former client that there is nothing to be afraid of in saying "I'm afraid." Admitting fear is the first step in overcoming that fear. And, there is nothing unmanly in saying the one scared you the most in life was little woman.

When lying down with a lying lamb occurs

SOMEONE ASKED ME HOW I could represent a person who's guilty.

I told 'em that was it was easy. My job was never to judge, but to uphold something called the Constitution.

It's the guy that planned to lie to a jury, however, that really got to me. When I told a judge in no uncertain terms of his intent, she told me I was stuck with him. No matter how hard I argued, the judge would not remove me from the case. I was forced to navigate a path I would not want to wish on my worst enemy.

I can't reveal details because of confidentiality concerns, but my client was accused of shooting someone who survived, and was not too shy about showing the chest wound to a camera crew filming the preliminary hearing results for the Six O'clock News.

My guy rejected the prosecutor's offer in this high publicity case. I requested a jury trial. In the United States, a person is presumed innocent and it's the burden of the district attorney to prove guilt beyond a reasonable doubt. I never had a problem with insuring a prosecutor prove his case in court. But the state's lawyer must prove guilt for each offense, and that's where one can often overplay his hand, particularly in "over-charging," believing a judge will acquit a defendant on the most serious charge, but convict on the ones a reasonable person would agree upon.

I'd consider a "compromise verdict" as a win for my client. With such a split decision, a defendant would be found guilty of lesser offenses and therefore face less time in prison. The most draconian sentence I ever saw imposed was 35-to-70-years for one of my clients. It was what I call "hard time," particularly when you're only 22 years of age at sentencing and you never physically injured anyone while brandishing a gun during a series of hold-ups.

So, I spoke to the press in this actual shooting case, planting the seeds for a defense that had decent chance of succeeding. It was based on the truth, and showed there was no intent to harm, but was the result of an accident the complainant brought on himself. I dug up evidence that showed the complainant had a propensity for violence. I documented it via a law suit alleging the "victim" resorted to violence in similar circumstances.

We got good coverage, but while firming up this defense with my client, he disagreed and told me he had been reading the law and learned that, not only did a defendant have a right to testify on his own behalf; he could tell a lie. He might have been right. But, looking him in the eye, I told him I would not <u>suborn</u> perjury and if he insisted, I would get out of his case and find someone else to represent him.

That's how I ended up asking a judge to remove me from the case. *"No, Mr. Contos,"* the jurist, one of the most learned in Philadelphia, said to me. She added that I would just be passing off a problem to another lawyer who would not know what I knew.

How can any honest person deal with such a dilemma? There is a provision in the law for this, and I thank my lucky stars I faced it only once. When you *know* a person is going to lie and you can't talk him out of it, the Code of

Ethics recommends you go forward with the defense, but ask the witness one and only one question when taking the witness stand. "What is your story?"

Don't ask any follow-up questions. Don't offer any attempts to clarify something on what is called "re-direct" examination of a witness. Lastly, when providing a closing argument, don't refer to anything the witness had testified to under oath. In essence, you give no credibility whatsoever to anything he might have said!

My client did the right thing. He never testified and therefore, never lied. Although he was found guilty, he got a standardized sentence as opposed to a maximum one he could have gotten.

I like to think that justice prevailed in the end. And, that's no lie.

Making Amends for Vietnam War in court

How do you say you're sorry to a people whose country you bombed in the name of peace and democracy?

What words can you use after saying that you are personally sorry for the Vietnam War and the mistakes our government made some 40 years ago?

A Native American once told me I could help myself by helping someone from Southeast Asia, and it got me thinking of ways to express my feelings after all these years. No, I won't return to Vietnam, despite what travel agencies are booking as a world-class tour, I said. Tunnels the Viet Cong used to flee American soldiers are now open for public view; you can spend a night at the Hanoi Hilton where American POWs were kept for years. You can return to Saigon, now Ho Chi Minh City, and try to rekindle the wild abandonment you had with some prostitute when you did not know if you would live to see another day so you drank and whored around all night.

Or, as my friend said as we huddled in sauna shared by men and women with clothing optional, I could look an Asian in the eye and express an awareness that I am only now realizing. We are the same. We are brothers. We are dependent on each other as all human beings are connected with their surroundings and the people they come in contact with today, tomorrow or yesterday.

"Try to help someone, maybe a family," the woman said in the steamy room. "I don't know of any," I said, drinking some cool water.

But that wasn't true. I remembered that I had once represented a young Asian man, charged with rape of a Cambodian woman in their apartment building. The jury found him not guilty, what I believed to be the correct verdict, but you would not have thought such an ending possible when the trial started.

You see, a good defense attorney will tell his client to "*get to*" a jury as soon as possible. In our case, it was at the "*ringing of the bell*," that moment in full view of the 12 jurors and two alternates when a judge asks the defendant to rise and solemnly demands to know how he (or she) wishes to plead.

"*Not guilty*" are words that I advised the young man to say loud enough for the number 14 juror in the far corner of the courtroom to plainly hear. A defendant cannot whisper these words. It would seem as if he wasn't sure of his innocence, and if that is the case, why should the fact-finder be any more certain upon hearing the person for the first, and in most criminal cases, the "*last*" time they hear his voice. (Unless you have an unusually gifted, articulate defendant, who has been thoroughly "*prepped*" to withstand the assault of even the most mediocre cross-examiner, you recommend to your client that there is little more to say after announcing a clear and concise "*NOT GUILTY*!"

I advised most defendants to assert their right *not* to testify, thereby placing the full burden on the prosecutor to proof guilty beyond a reasonable doubt. This was planned *before* the last juror took his seat. My client, who spoke no English, got to his feet as the judge addressed him. He remembered to turn slightly toward the jury box and look in the jury's direction, also as planned.

> *What came out of his mouth was anything but reassuring of his inno-cence. He shouted at the top of his lungs, making a unintelligible sound that made me cringe and want to hide beneath the defense table and raise a white flag of surrender.*
>
> *He yelled "not guilty" in the Cambodian language! No one, I mean no one on the jury, or even in the courtroom, knew what that young man had just blurted out.*

I forgot to instruct him through an interpreter to practice his English at this crucial time in the one and only trial of his life. Instead of projecting a confidence in his innocence, he sent a signal that was confusing at best, and at worst, made a bad impression that could turn someone presuming him innocent to wondering why he even asked for a trial following his now evident show of guilt.

The trial, however, went well for the defense, and I was able to score points against the young woman who never told the assistant district attorney that she suffered from seizures. It all came out under my cross-examination, making it seem that the prosecutor was trying to hide something. In addition, she had suffered a seizure outside her apartment building the day this incident occurred and woke up in her second floor bedroom with my client breathing heavily while standing over her.

We found witnesses that said he carried her from the pavement outside into the apartment complex and performed a needed humanitarian service for her.

She, however, testified he raped her. But there was no physical evidence, no corroborating witnesses, and she had to admit that she was unable to recall any details of an assault when I pressed her. In other words, she told the jury she had been raped after finding herself in bed with a man not her husband at her side, unable to remember how she got there, or how this man was able to breach her most private room. What she ended up telling her husband shortly after finding the two together was anybody's guess. He never came to court and the jury took notice.

I would like to say that my client and I became fast friends after the not guilty verdict, but it just wouldn't be true. However, I did become quite close with the interpreter, a short Vietnamese man who translated multiple Asian languages as well as dialects. We would joke about my defendant's outburst to the jury and we always had kind words for each other the days, weeks and years that passed.

Shaking hands with him made me feel I made a life-long friend. He made me feel we were family.

He also reminded me of a *"Kit Carson"* scout that worked with me, with our platoon, serving as translator and guide in the *"bush."* I never really had a chance to thank that scout for his help, and for his cheery attitude in the field, particularly in the mornings when he greeted me with a smile and the energy to make the best of each day.

I now believe that my translator friend became that scout I never was able to thank. I had tried to make amends many years ago and it wasn't until that moment in a synthetic *"sweat lodge"* that some spirit arose and finally brought it to my attention, finally brought it home.

I felt healed. I felt forgiven.

Tattoo Tests Tale to Tell the Truth

A TATTOO CAN READILY IDENTIFY someone, and sometimes one can become the key to the guilt or innocence of a man facing the wrath of a woman he may have wronged.

A tattoo figured prominently in the last case I tried as a public defender in Philadelphia. I didn't know it was to be my final court battle. Post-traumatic stress disorder (PTSD) had taken its toll on me, and I thought two weeks of treatment at an inpatient veterans' clinic would cure the rage and anger that had led to three near-brawls in the courtroom. Turns out I needed the full 10-week course and a complete resignation from 20 years of stress as a trial attorney.

The Philadelphia District Attorney had charged my client with robbery as well as harassment and stalking in a case we were to try before a judge hearing the facts without a jury. The police report said he had repeatedly called his ex-girlfriend at her place of work and eventually stole a cell phone from her.

I wanted him to plead guilty when I got the charges lowered to just misdemeanors. In addition, he would have had to pay for the phone. He refused the offer, demanding to go to trial and get a chance to walk out of court free with only probation.

Violent, ugly visions popped into my head. I saw myself pushing my client's head through the flat-white-colored wall in the tiny conference room cut out of a section of the courtroom. I yelled at him and asked whom he thought the judge would believe, him or the articulate girl who would have all the sympathy in the world when she told her story as outlined in her statement to the police?

I told him that a misdemeanor conviction would not keep him from getting a job. Most employers ask only if you've been convicted of a felony, the more serious offense. "Hell," I said, "you could tell them the truth if you pleaded guilty to a minor offense to get away from an ex-girlfriend who was out for revenge for breaking up with her."

"That's exactly what happened, Mr. Contos," he said. "And I won't plead guilty to something I didn't do."

The trial went as I expected. The young, attractive African America woman was not only sympathetic, she spoke with a ring of truth while testifying. She said he had constantly called her house and her place of work. Despite her pleas with him to stop, he'd increased the calls and even threatened to confront her at work, she said, if he couldn't get his way.

> *However, her story started to unravel under cross-examination. She produced no evidence to support her allegation. There were no phone records, no recordings of a castoff or angry ex-lover, no other witnesses.*

> *It turned out that the defendant did confront her at work, and that he did take the cell phone from her. But she said it was his cell phone that he had given to her when their relationship was healthy and loving.*

I knew we had raised reasonable doubt when I asked a question my client requested I pose when whispering to me at the defense table and she was just about to step down from the witness stand.

"Yes, I do have a tattoo," she answered. "Yes, it's his name," she added, nodding in the direction of the man she accused.

My client testified persuasively that she was the real "stalker" after he broke off the relationship. I introduced "good character" evidence, which, *in and of itself*, could raise a reasonable doubt for a not-guilty verdict, and the judge acquitted him of all charges, explaining that he could not decide who was telling the truth and that therefore, by law, he must find in favor of the defendant.

To this day, I believe the judge reasoned that the woman had more to lose in the couple's breakup because she had so much more invested in keeping the relationship intact. Mainly, she had his name forever marked on her arm.

Happy Mothers' Day, Poor Little Thérèse

(The following is a composite tale of women I represented in court)

How could I – a mother of two with a 10-year drug problem – be facing a life sentence for something stupid I did at the local Rite Aid store?

I tried to steal deodorant and toothpaste and got caught. I'd been in that same store over a year earlier, and they let me go when I tried to take something. I was wearing a different jacket, not like the one I had from my boyfriend this time. This jacket had a needle in the pocket. I used the needle earlier that day and had hoped to get high with him later that night. How was I supposed to know I'd poke myself with it when getting arrested?

> Yeah, stupid me. I had my hand in my pocket where I kept the syringe when the store clerk – some overweight geek wearing glasses and smelling too much of Old Spice after shave – grabbed me from behind and yanked me by my hair. He lied at the preliminary hearing, saying he grabbed me by the arm. No, he pulled me by my hair and I almost left my feet as my whole head got yanked toward his fat and oily face.

I barely had time to stay on my feet and try to find my balance when I pulled my hand from my pocket. The exposed needle had punctured the web of my hand. You know, that spot between the base of the thumb and the index finger. I don't know how I did it, but I got it out of my skin with just the one hand and was able to hold it in the palm of my hand as I turned and swung my arm to protect myself while also trying to steady myself.

Once again, the clerk lied about what happened. He said I was trying to stab him with the needle. How could I? He was like two feet away from me and I couldn't get close enough to him once I got out of his grasp and swung around. The manager was right there, standing in front of me, holding me as I bumped into him. He had circled around the aisle I had last walked, pinning me between himself and the clerk. He saw how far away I was from the geek. Yet he kept his mouth shut when the judge held me on the charge of attempted murder.

Little ole me. One hundred pounds soaking wet in my 4-foot, 10-inch frame. Held for trying to kill the geek, a 200-pound gorilla who nearly decapitated me when he pulled me from behind.

They said I had hepatitis B and that I was trying to spread it to him with the point of the needle. I once had Hepatitis B, but not anymore. The test they did at the Philadelphia Prison was a false positive. I could prove it if I could find the name of the doctor or nurse or whomever it was that told me of the results. All the DA (district attorney) had in her file was the first report which she read to the judge with no challenge by my court-appointed lawyer, not that he knew anything about it. I never told him until now.

But even if we could get the charge thrown out, my lawyer said I'd still be facing what they call a *mandatory minimum* sentence of 25-years-to-life. Twenty-five years-to-life! Can you imagine what that means? You have a better chance of becoming canonized than you do of getting out of prison alive when you're sentenced at my age, 39. I'd be 64 by the time I'm freed from jail. Sixty-four. Remember the song, *"When I'm 64?"* "Will you still be sending me a valentine, birthday greetings, bottle of wine?" You wouldn't have to send me a thing. I'd be long dead by then.

My mother died at 54; my father, of whom I met only once, never made it to age 40. Both were alcoholics. I got their genes and going to jail for 25 years would be like imposing a death sentence on me.

You see, I'm what you call a "repeat offender." someone who has repeated the same crimes over and over. The crimes started out as misdemeanors, but soon got to be felonies, the more serious offenses that carried much stiffer sentences.

I got arrested for drugs and shoplifting. That's it. One time I got caught selling reefer. I had some crack on me and got initially charged with sale of both marijuana and crack, even though I never sold a lick of crack ever. I'd take a lie detector test to prove it, too, but my lawyer was able to get the crack charge thrown out!

It's the shoplifting that did me in, said my lawyer. Here in Pennsylvania, they have a law which makes shoplifting a serious offense. The first time, they only charge you with a summary offense. That's like spitting on the sidewalk, they say, but I never heard of anyone being charged for it. I guess it's on the books, though.

A second offense will get you a misdemeanor charge. Now, that's more serious than a summary offense. Both are called by the legal name of "retail thefts." ("Retail theft" — I thought that applied to the type of store a shoplifter would frequent, like a department store where they sold things at a retail price.)

Remember Kresge's? That's where I first took something. I was about 6 or 7 and the woman who caught me grilled me, wanting to know where I went to school and who my second-grade teacher was. I told her everything. "Sister Josephine Francis wouldn't like to hear one of her students was stealing, would she?" the clerk asked me, my head pointed to the old wooden polished floors, afraid to look up and make any type of eye contact.

Guilty. I'm guilty as sin, I thought. Worse yet, I got caught being guilty as sin and that sin is about to be made public. They're going to tell my teacher and I will go to hell. Not right away, but I'd be on the path to hell, just as sure as I was on the path to receiving my first Holy communion, if I could ever turn back the clock and never, never again take something that didn't belong to me.

Please God. Please Jesus. Help me! I'm scared. I'm afraid!

The lady, a tall, thin woman with dark brown hair pulled back with a small beret at the top, stood in front of me for what seemed like hours, but was only a few seconds. I thought I would die in her presence. If there was hole in the floor of Woolworth's I'd jump right in and dig my way all the way to China.

"Promise me you won't do this again," I heard the woman say. Her voice sounded so very far away, as if she was in another room and was speaking to me through some sort of chamber. I didn't comprehend what she was saying at first. But, then I said, "I promise." I said it with all the heart-filled sincerity I could muster from the very bottom of wherever truth and goodness resided in side of me at the time.

I don't know if I cried. I might have. I don't remember tears in my eyes, as the woman told me to turn around and leave the store. She said she wouldn't report me this time, but if she heard from anyone that I took something again, she'd let the nuns know right away.

I left and did not break the Seventh commandment, "Thou Shalt Not Steal," until my second daughter was born and by then the father of my children got me hooked on drugs. I'd forgotten what happened to me in Woolworth's until just now. It never came up those times I was shoplifting the past 15 years.

I done wrong by my kids, but they're better off without a mother like me for now. If I can ever get into one of those long-term treatment programs with long-term follow-up in a woman's halfway house, I might be able to control my problem, and get back to being a real mother for them. I know I can do it. I feel that I got God's help now, and, somehow, that will make all the difference.

But under the Three Strikes and You're out Law, I'm facing the maximum sentence. Yeah, you read that right. The mandatory minimum of 25-year-to-life is both a minimum and a maximum for me. Twenty-five years is a maximum to anyone who must give up all those years to pay for his or her crime. Look at it this way. Twenty-five years is eight years short of the life-span of Jesus Christ. Twenty-five years is more than half the life-span of St. Francis of Assisi who died at age 45.

And, it's more than the entire life-span of the one they call the "Little Flower," the Catholic saint I was named for, Thérèse of Lisieux, who was acclaimed as "the greatest saint of modern times." She did the little things in life that made her what she became, a saint who died when she was only 24-years old. All I did was "little things" in my life; never did anything really bad, like commit murder or some other mortal sin or anything like that, you know.

Twenty-five years for a tube of toothpaste and an Arrid roll-on antiperspirant.

Jeez. What's the world coming to?

All-women jury renders "unknown" verdict

THE ONE AND ONLY TIME I stood before an all-women jury, I ended up asking for a mistrial after the judge and prosecutor entered the jury deliberation room without my knowledge and in violation of the sequestration rule to safeguard against jury tampering.

The judge, a prosecutorial-oriented jurist, denied my request for a new trial, and I objected for the record. No lawyer or a judge is permitted access to a jury once a panel is sworn in, and none can enter the jury room while deliberations have started. On learning such a breach, I described step-by-step how such actions prejudiced my client.

The defendant was charged with burglarizing a neighbor's home. The victim, a young attractive woman, had testified someone had entered her bedroom while she was asleep and stole money. She said she awoke and saw the intruder as he was leaving her second floor window, and recognized the assailant as a neighbor of whom she knew since childhood.

The complainant was sympathetic and appeared credible while testifying for the prosecutor. The defendant denied committing the crime. But I advised him not to testify. He was a big guy, over six-feet tall, with a muscular built. He was single and unemployed, with a record for car thefts and shop-lifting. Under Pennsylvania law, he could be impeached for crimes of "dishonesty" if he testified. Receiving stolen goods, retail theft and unauthorized use of a vehicle are among what lawyers call *"crimen falsi"* offenses. If the defendant took the stand, the prosecutor would introduce the prior convictions to show he's not worthy of belief. His record, however, would not be revealed if he remained silent. (Note: a person convicted of such heinous crimes as murder and rape would not be subject to the same rule. Those offenses have no bearing on one's honesty, according to the law, and a jury would never learn of *crimen falsi* impeachment evidence if a convicted rapist and/or a murderer decided to testify.)

The entire defense rested on my ability to "shake" the testimony of the eyewitness, who became more likeable, credible and confident in her ID with each word she spoke to smiling members of the jury. I planned to focus on the dark surroundings, the limited amount of time to witness things, and the basic questions highlighting an inability to see. If she stuck to her self-confident demeanor, however, there would be little if any reasonable doubt to ask the jury to focus on.

The judge had ordered a break in the proceedings when the prosecutor finished with the witness. Something happened then that changed the dynamics of the case. I had repeatedly asked the assistant district attorney for a copy of the initial police report that had not been provided earlier. "I don't have one in the file," she said. I finally approached the detective in charge of the case. He was a no-nonsense type of cop who had a good reputation for honesty. He had a copy of the report and upon reading it, I saw a major inconsistency that could prove fatal to the prosecutor case.

The first cop on the scene wrote that an *"unknown"* assailant had committed the crime. He got that information from the witness. He would not have used the abbreviation for "unknown" had the woman told him otherwise. Using the report, I confronted the witness with her "prior inconsistent" statement. I watched the juror's faces – one woman after another — as the physical report was "published," that is, given to each juror to read. There was silence in the court room. No testimony was offered as one by one the jurors looked first at the report, and then the witness, in what I had hoped would be a different light.

Here was evidence, I'd later argue, that the victim's testimony was not reliable, and that the correct version of the truth was in the police report, the one the prosecutor had not provided me despite repeated requests.

When I heard that this same prosecutor had had contact with the jurors I believed she was trying to circumvent the justice system. I believe she had tried to do the same when failing to provide defense counsel with the police report.

I don't know what she said in the closed jury room. She and the judge entered to escort a child out of the room. It seems one of the jurors could not get a baby-sitter the second day of deliberations and had brought her child with her. The jury could not work with such a distraction. All 12 needed to deliberate since the alternates had been dismissed. A woman working somewhere in the Philadelphia court system eventually took charge of the child allowing the jurors to deliberate.

How could I trust this jury to do the right thing now? I never had all women on a jury before. Would there be some sort of reverse discrimination against me and the male defendant? Would they hold it against me for not helping to seat the juror in need of child care? What subtle or not so subtle messages could any have gleaned from their contact with the female prosecutor?

All of these thoughts went through my mind as a verdict was reached, and I stood in the courtroom with my client, head bowed waiting for the foreperson to make her announcement. I had already started writing an appeal as I focused on that chilling moment every trial lawyer experiences when he or she hears the first words of a jury's collective decision spoken: "*We, the jury, find the defendant . . .*" There always seems to be a pause at that point. To this day, I cannot listen without my heart beating fast and hard in my throat.

My one and only all-woman jury, however, did what I believed was the right thing! They acquitted the defendant, and freed him as the alto-pitched voice offered a resounding "Not Guilty" verdict. Thank God a gender-neutral justice prevailed!

Truth revealed in trial despite the lawyer

A "DEAD-DOG-LOSER" IS THE NAME trial lawyers gave to cases no one expected you to win in court. I had a few of them and always tried my best to get a defendant to plead guilty before making a fool of myself and him by calling his case "ready" for trial.

There was one case, however, that I couldn't escape from, and I ended up trying it to a jury despite my best efforts not to.

Many lawyers would duck these type of cases, in hopes of tiring out a civilian witness who usually had to take time off from work to come to the courthouse. Two or three continuances could wear out even the most civic-minded person. But then there was always those who would appear in court each and every time an assistant district attorney subpoenaed them. You couldn't escape those diehards no matter what you did.

Public defenders could avoid these cases through continuances knowing that another lawyer would end up with the loser once they rotated from that courtroom or judge they had been assigned to. A continuance would stretch over a six week period which was time enough for another attorney to face the defendant refusing to plea-bargain.

I never ducked any cases. I might have seen it as guy thing. I had been to Vietnam during the war and I figured I could handle just about anything a judge could throw at me during a trial by a jury. At least no one would be shooting at me no matter how bad my closing argument would be!

Several attorneys who represented this one fellow kept ducking the case that I was eventually assigned to. After reading the police report, I could understand. The case was a *"caught inside burglary."* There were no defense for such criminal acts and I kind of figured the case would be a "slow guilty plea" when I put it up for trial, if you know what I mean.

The owner of the building testified that he caught my client in his car-repair shop early in the morning. He held the miscreant with a baseball bat threatening to do him harm should he try to run away before the police got to them.

My client told a different story, however. His version of the truth was that he never went inside the building but was stopped when he walked along side of it. It was dark out, and he said he was going to apply for a job at a site immediately adjacent to the victim's building in the early morning.

He told the story with quite a conviction and I figured I could let him tell his story before the jury found him guilty and allowed the judge to sentence him.

And that is why I told his story in my opening statement. It was something I had not done in my practice of the law up until that point. And that is to tell the story as if I was the defendant talking to his lawyer.

The trial looked bad for my client but then it kind of "broke my way." That is, facts my client said in private were slowly revealed in public during the course of the trial's give and take, particularly when I'd cross-exam the prosecution witnesses.

A police officer had stated that the neighboring building had a hiring process open to the public early that morning The only way to approach the building was to walk past the defendant's place, he said.

The cop also helped when he said he knew the victim because of previous encounters with him and his place of business. The man had been burglarized before and that this was the first time anyone had been caught.

This testimony was in direct conflict with what the complainant had testified to earlier. I made a note of the contradiction and brought it up during my closing argument. I highlighted this fact as well as the exact words the victim had used after he said he had discovered my client in his shop.

He said *"Go ahead and make my day,"* as he held the bat to my client's head.

My client said that the man had actually held him at gunpoint after ushering him into the building upon confronting him outside. In other words, he forced my client into the building and then called the police, stating that he caught my guy inside.

Clint Eastwood made that line famous, you may recall. In a Dirty Harry movie. Eastwood pointed the gun at the perp and said ""*Make my day.*" No one would use that term while holding a bat, I had argued. He held a gun to the defendant's head but refused to say that.

My client had sabotaged the case when the prosecution had rested her case, however. I had expected the defendant to testify in his own defense and had prepped him for it. Now he told me he wasn't going to take the witness stand and the slim chance I thought I had developed finally dissolved. I told the jury what my client had said during the opening statement and I believed they expected to hear from him, even though I never said he would in those many words.

Luckily, I had the law with me. You see, a defendant has the right at a criminal trial not to testify. He can assert his Fifth Amendment privilege not to incriminate himself.

As importantly, the law forbids a prosecutor from making any comment of his lack of testifying. It would create an automatic mistrial. The case would be thrown out if one could prove there was prosecutorial misconduct in referring to the criminal defendant not testifying.

"Not guilty" jury foreman announced several hours after the deliberation. I had been standing with my client when the judge ordered him to stand and the assistant DA threw her file to the desk in disgust with the verdict announcement. The judge admonished the lawyer — a nice-looking slender woman in her early 30s —and she simply pushed her chair in, without raising her eyes to the judge or to the jury that refused to believe the so-called victim.

A dead-dog-loser had turned into a winner!

My client had told the truth and it set him free despite the lack of faith by his lawyer. I never forgot that lesson and I pray to God I never will.

The truth can indeed set us all free.

Don Quixote battles PTSD in Philly courts

I NEVER FELT MORE LIKE Don Quixote than when I represented a woman charged with a crime.

And while I didn't want it, I'd feel called to *"champion"* her, even when it cost me my reputation, my sanity and my very career as a trial attorney.

I provided dignity to clients as a public defender, especially the women. Heroin addicts became respected ladies who needed someone to tell their story to a Court system most were unaccustomed in doing battle. Many with only a minimum education became learned seers who knew more of surviving in the world than many with MAs and Ph.Ds.

I took up the sword and fought like there was no tomorrow. Two women, both White, come to my mind. Both got lured by heavy drugs. One faced a mandatory sentence for purchasing a gun for a drug supplier who just happened to be a felon. She had cervical cancer and simply wanted to be with her family — and child — for treatment, and not receive it out of the Women's Facility of the State Prison in Muncie, PA.

The other was out on the streets, having gotten high with her boyfriend when she put the needle into a jacket for later use and went to a Rite Aid drug store to get deodorant and other goods.

She stuffed them into the jacket — the pocket holding the needle — with plans to walk out without paying. In other words, be a shoplifter. She did it before. At the same Rite Aid.

Someone at the store recognized her, she told me when visiting her in prison several months after her arrest. Yes Virginia, there really is incarceration for people with criminal records, despite what others want you to believe. She sat in jail some four months before her case was "*called to trial.*" I requested a continuance for further corroboration of her story.

See, two men stopped her in the store. A manager grabbed her from the rear and a clerk got to her up front. She tried to leave and resisted as they held her. She claimed one held her by her hair. The other pulled the stolen items from her jacket pocket.

She clutched the needle as it spilled from her jacket, cutting her hand, she told me, showing a slight scar on her finger. One of the men saw the needle and claimed she twisted it and positioned it so that she could "*stab*" 'em with it. She never did. One man testified that she actually swung her arm in attempt — he wanted the court to believe, was — to inject 'em with a what an ADA would later argue, a "*tainted*" needle.

While placed in prison, a test showed she had Hepatitis B.

A specially assigned assistant district attorney (ADA) was appointed to prosecute her, with an initial charge of attempted murder.

"*It was a false positive,*" the woman told me of the test. She claimed she had proof from some doctor that she wasn't "*contagious.*" I use the word *contagious* for lack of a better medical understanding. I immediately got an investigation started to confirm this to share it with the ADA, a woman I had worked with before and respected.

The case came to Court and I advised the young prosecutor of the woman's claim to show a lack of intent to cause such grave injury. I went into detail, sharing my information in hopes of securing a plea for a lesser offense than aggravated assault, which would have required my client serve a minimum of five years in jail, mainly because of her record. A long one made up of drug possession cases and lots of retail thefts (shoplifting).

"When did she learn it was a false positive?" the prosecutor asked, refusing to lower an offer of 5-to-10 years. I started to tell her, and she let slip her reason for the question. If my client had t not known it was a false positive until after being arrested and sent to jail, then the ADA could prove *"intent"* at the time of she was caught shoplifting.

I went ballistic. I flash-backed to Vietnam. Suffered perhaps the worst episode of Post-Traumatic Stress that has ever surfaced in my life.

I reverted to the first lieutenant who realized a member of his platoon was placed into immediate danger. By me. In my efforts to help, I made it worse.

"Get out of here," I yelled to the ADA at the bar of the Court. *"Get the fuck outta here,"* I added through a clenched jaw while pointing to a door leading out of the courtroom. A sheriff had just brought the defendant into the courtroom and I felt justified in demanding the prosecutor leave so I could maintain confidentiality with my client at the defense table in the open Court.

Several lawyers, defendants, and witnesses with other cases, as well as police sat stunned as they watched my *"over-the-top"* behavior. I didn't care. Instead, I *"played"* to them all, pointing out that the ADA — straight out of what's called the *"Habitual Offender Unit,"* was — in my opinion — trying to get a conviction for the worst offense, and not seek justice.

I stopped practicing about a month later. Got into a few more "*blow ups*" with prosecutors while awaiting treatment for PTSD (post-traumatic stress disorder), and clearing my schedule of trial work for a month. That's the amount of time I thought I would need to "*cure*" myself.

It's been years since I stopped practicing and left. I'm not sure what happened to either woman. Other lawyers were appointed to "*champion*" their causes. Today, I liken myself to a Don Quixote with a foolish hope back then to right all wrongs and tilt at windmills — "*they might be giants!*" I like what I see in the mirror and, more importantly, the dreamer still within me . . .

Here's to you, my *Delcinea*!

(I started writing a Blog for WordPress about a year after I stopped representing clients in the courtroom. I simply titled it "Contoveros" after my father who had passed away some 30 years earlier.

I learned how to meditate from a psychologist who taught veterans with PTSD (Post-Traumatic Stress Disorder) how to deal with their demons through a process called mindfulness while we met with her at the Veterans Medical Center in Coatesville, Pennsylvania.

Writing was helpful in dealing with PTSD. It offered a chance to reflect and offer compassion to myself for anger issues a kid growing up in Brewerytown would be exposed to. I put this book together for my grandson, Jameson, so that he could see what problems his "Pappou" had to overcome.

I figured I'd end it with a final salute to my favorite son, Nicholas Alexander Contos, who I acknowledged on his 18th birthday.)

Post Script

Nicholas: Happy 18th Birthday Son

"*He's a real banana head*," the doctor who delivered you pronounced right after your birth Nicholas Alexander Contos. You looked more like a "*prune*" with all those wrinkles; kinda like an aging Dwight Eisenhower or a Winston Churchill, but with a lot more wrinkles.

Today, March 2, 2010, your 18th birthday, you blossomed into a handsome young man, strong of mind and body with a heart as big as the place in which you came from, Cleveland, Ohio.

I remember having to change you, fumbling around, taking you from your birth mother, Angie, in the middle of the night, rocking you, burping you and patting your back. The whole time forgetting to brush my teeth creating such a "yucky" feeling all day.

I nearly broke my arm some months later when I forgot to secure you in a portable "chair" I placed on the bay window-sill. You wriggled out and started to fall to the hard floor below when I dove, hit the dining room floor with my elbow and cushioned your blow in my arms. What a catch. And what an injury. Still feel the pain on days it rains.

First day in school a photographer from our local newspaper captured you in a picture that spread across five of the six columns of the front page. A reporter was doing a story on a classmate who just happened to be standing in line behind you as you were following your first grade teacher into Conshohocken

Elementary School. That picture is now framed and displayed in the dining room, not far from the spot I "caught" you some years earlier.

The living room offers visitors a look at a 14-year-old Nicholas hugging his *"birth mother,"* meeting her for the first time since she permitted us to raise you in March of 1992. You are all smiles, and look comfortable, and seem to be as well-adjusted as a banana mixed with a scoop of ice cream in a banana split.

You became one of a hundred in the photo showing you with other members of Concert Chorus for Montgomery County, displaying your singing talents in Middle School and High School. But, you wanted to become a *"rock star,"* grew your hair long, learned to play a guitar and formed a band with two girls and two guys with you as a lead singer. Can't forget the holes in the knee of the jeans you all seem to be wearing in the picture I took.

At 16, you flashed your best smile for a driver's license, and were lucky to avoid having to pose for a police *"mug shot"* following the series of car accidents and minor run-ins with the local authorities. I asked myself, why is he following in my footsteps? I found it hard to stay out of trouble, too. And kinda knew it was part of the growing process, the *"risk-taking,"* the testing of life boundaries at a certain age.

Today, you officially become a man. At least in the eyes of the law.

I love you, and want you to know that you'll always be my favorite son. What's that? You say that you're my only son?

Happy birthday, Nicholas. Here's dad, proudly smiling at you kid!

<u>Comments on "Nicholas: Happy 18th Birthday, Son"</u>

Colleen DuBois: This is a heartwarming tribute to your son Michael. Thank you for sharing it with us.

Bliss bait: This is SOOOOO DEAR! Happy Birthday Nicholas!!!! What a grand time. You're at! And thank you for sharing this, Michael. Cheers and Namaste.

Nick: Thanks for the birthday wishes.

But, now I want my dad to write about the Rooster who will be 1 yr. old March 12, 2010.

Wolf Shades: What a tribute! Happy Birthday Nicholas! I know you're probably as awesome as your dad says. Know why? Cause the best people are born in or around the beginning of March. (My birthday was yesterday, is how I know). *grinning*

Cheers!

Nick: Thank you so much for the birthday wishes…and I am more awesome than my father says… Ha-ha. It's nice to hear that I'm not the only one with a birthday in early march…so happy birthday to you as well!

Kim: Parenting is one of the best journeys in life, isn't it? Happy Birthday Nicholas!

Nick: thank you so much for the birthday wishes!

Words We Never Said: *smile*!

To Nicholas:

Happy birthday!!!!!!! – You will make a great man, I just know it!

I would say 'make your Dad proud' but the real thing to remember is to act in a way that you will be proud of yourself – your Father's pride will be a 'given' (Dads are good that way.)

Being able to have something you feel you can always tell a Mother is not a bad idea either…

(Just sayin')

I was about to give you some advice about going out to party for your birthday until I remembered that – in the States – you are not legal to drink when we are here in Canada.

So – even IF you won't be going to the bar for another couple years – hopefully you can a least have share a beer with your Dad and reflect on the whole 'man' thing *smile*

All the best to you Mr. Nicholas!

Nick: I laughed at this when you said I should go to the bar…I would love to if I was old enough here…my father just told me maybe we can share some Vino… (if you don't know what that is it is red wine) but if you read any of his blogs about going to Greece he might have left out the fact that the drinking age there is 16…and when I was there I had my first beer it was a Heineken…

The End